Why We Need
Girlfriends

A Bible Study for Women

Why We Need Girlfriends

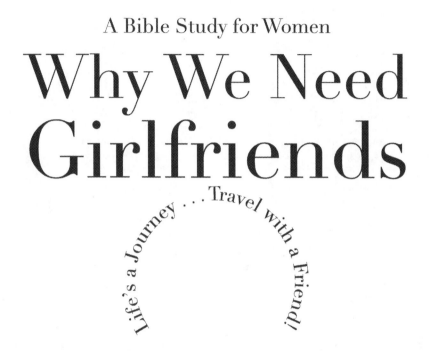

Life's a Journey . . . Travel with a Friend!

Frankie Sherman

WESTBOW®
PRESS
A DIVISION OF THOMAS NELSON
& ZONDERVAN

WestBow Press books may be ordered through booksellers or by contacting:

WestBow Press
A Division of Thomas Nelson & Zondervan
1663 Liberty Drive
Bloomington, IN 47403
www.westbowpress.com
1 (866) 928-1240

ISBN: 978-1-4908-3042-1 (sc)

Library of Congress Control Number: 2014904991

Printed in the United States of America.

WestBow Press rev. date: 03/20/2014

This book is lovingly dedicated to my mom—the first Elizabeth
in my life who lived the Word before me.
To Jan McCray, who taught me to love the Word.
And to the Glory Girls—you are glorious!

Contents

Acknowledgments

Beth Beutler, my editor in SC, you inspired and encouraged me to be a better writer. You are the best.

Raydell Tedder, my proofreader, I appreciate your respect and knowledge of the English language.

Amy Tedder of *AT Your Design,* the inspiration behind the layout design, your vision amazes me.

To all the women in the churches across America who have invited me to share this message—we are girlfriends forever.

My girlfriends at Laurens First Baptist Church, for your amazing support …you are loved.

Above all, my heavenly Father, who created friendship and calls me friend.

About This Book

Things seemed much simpler when I was a young girl growing up in the South. It was the early 60s, long before the women's movement, Oprah, and text messaging. Back then, the women in my circle of influence weren't concerned about finding their place in the world. They believed that just being born a woman was a privilege!

Most of these amazing women worked outside the home, but it is their work in the kingdom of God that I most admire. Right before my eyes they demonstrated the beauty of friendship.

In those days of my youth I witnessed the God-given joy of *being* a woman and the joy of being *with* women. My mentors taught me that I was twice blessed—once for being born female and again for experiencing the friendship of women.

I was privileged to be among women who were secure in their femininity and believed that being a woman was something to *celebrate.* I witnessed with delight how they confided in and connected with each other, and sometimes collapsed into laughter over the silliest things.

These unique women demonstrated a valuable life lesson to me: *I would need girlfriends,* because life is meant to be *shared.*

Today, I am much older, and life is far more complicated. What I learned as a young girl remains true: women need girlfriends. That is the heart and soul of this book—because friendship is God's idea.

Over the next seven weeks we will discover that:

- God's timing is perfect.
- Friendship is God's idea.
- Friendship is God's unique gift for us to enjoy.

- Friendship helps us reach others for Christ.
- God has established guidelines for healthy friendships.
- God has called each of us to be an Elizabeth and a Mary of the 21st century.

We will use the acronym F.R.I.E.N.D. to guide us on our way. Each week, you'll be provided four lessons to study throughout the week. Each will give you an opportunity for:

- Sightseeing: investigating God's Word and learning more about the journey;
- Conversations: sharing thoughts and applications;
- Travel Diary: a place for you to take the concepts to heart;
- Traveling Mercies: a guided prayer;
- Snapshot: a short, memorable thought to help you remember the concept.
- Travel Tips with verses recommended for memorization and thoughts to enhance your study.

Pack Your Bags

Welcome aboard Girlfriend! I am so glad that you will be taking this journey with me. For the next few weeks, we will explore the lives and the relationship of two incredible women—Elizabeth, the mother of John the Baptist, and Mary, the mother of Jesus.

We have many miles to travel. The scenery is breathtaking and the traveling companions are people you will never forget.

Considering my driving record, I have invited the heavenly Father to take the driver's seat. Be advised—He is not interested in shortcuts. He desires this trip to be life-changing.

Our journey begins in the Old Testament long before the Messiah was born. It was a desperate time in history. We'll move forward to the New Testament, where in the temple we'll meet an angel named Gabriel, and an old priest named Zechariah. Then it's off to Galilee where a young woman will discover her life's calling. Finally, we'll end at my favorite place, the home of Elizabeth.

For our journey, I have used the New International Version (NIV) with occasional passages from other versions. However, I invite you to use the one that will most enhance your journey. In fact, you may want to try several versions!

I also recommend keeping a journal during your study time. It is always wise to record what God is doing in our lives. Finally, record Scripture verses you want to memorize on index cards for easy reference.

The study is written in an interactive format to enhance your learning and application of Scripture. Each week the study will provide four devotionals with recommended Scripture reading and questions to help you dig deeper. For the most part, we will camp in the first chapter of the Book of Luke. To receive the most benefit from your journey, I pray that you will make this study and time with the Lord a priority.

Like many sightseers, you might be tempted to do all of the week's lessons at once. However, as an experienced traveler, let me encourage you to study each lesson one day at a time. Allow yourself time to think about what you have read, and journal what God is teaching you.

Our ultimate destination is to become women like Elizabeth and Mary—women who prepared for the coming of the Messiah. During our time together, we will discover exactly what that means.

I feel privileged to be your guide. So, if you're ready, let's go pack our bags and get ready for a wonderful adventure. I've been on this journey for a while now, and I can tell you it is the trip of a lifetime!

Frankie

ITINERARY

Week One

> **Day 1**—The Road Trip to Friendship Begins with God
>
> **Day 2**—Traveling Companions
>
> **Day 3**—Journaling with Jesus
>
> **Day 4**—Don't Forget the Map

TRAVEL TIP

> *"He traveled through that area, speaking many words of encouragement to the people"* (Acts 20:2a NIV).

WEEK 1, DAY 1
THE ROAD TRIP TO FRIENDSHIP BEGINS WITH GOD

SIGHTSEEING

Before *Why We Need Girlfriends* became a book, it was a weekend retreat study. Creating the material was quite a process, requiring hours of research and intense writing. Upon completion, and after teaching it across the country, I was pleased that women were grasping its purpose—that friendship is God's idea! No more late nights alone with commentaries and biblical scholars. Now I could have the fun of sharing what I learned. Hallelujah!

Or, so I thought. I'd forgotten that God never leaves us in our comfort zone for long. One phone call would interrupt my road trip, and in many ways, change its direction. (Thank goodness the commentaries were still on my desk.)

I was invited to lead a women's retreat at a church on the friendship of Mary and Elizabeth. The director of the retreat called and asked that I also include a session on our friendship with God. I almost dropped the phone. *Friendship with God?* What? Didn't she know that God is the sovereign LORD, the Almighty, and the Holy One? One of my sessions included *revering* God! Help her, Lord, I silently prayed, hoping He would convict her about the idea of relating to Him in such a casual manner.

As I listened to her, I thought to myself, I have been a believer all my life. I know God as Savior, Redeemer, and Lord, but as Friend? I had many friends. Did I want to consider God in such an informal way? I didn't think so.

I told her I would pray about it. And, I did.

CONVERSATIONS

Before I go on, if you are amazed that I had a hard time relating to God as a friend, allow me to explain. Perhaps you can relate.

I grew up without a father in the home. This left a hole in my heart, an empty place that only a dad can fill. Children need both a mother and a father. While that isn't always possible, it is the ideal. In my situation, I looked to God to be the father I didn't have and allowed Him that primary role in my life. To think of Him as *friend* felt as if it would diminish His holiness, and show a lack of respect. I couldn't bear that.

Instead of giving the caller a lesson on God's sovereignty, I went before the Lord with my dilemma. He knew my background and my need. I relied upon the promise in Jeremiah 29:13 NIV that says, "You will seek me and find me when you seek me with all of your heart."

God led me to a scripture that I had read a number of times, but this time I saw it in a new light. James 2:23 says, "Abraham believed God, and it was reckoned to him as righteousness, and he was called the friend of God (RVS)." James was quoting from Isaiah 41:8. Interestingly, this was not Abraham's assessment of his relationship with God, nor how he thought about God. The great, almighty, all-powerful, ever-present, all-knowing God was the One who made this statement!

As believers, we have entered into a covenant just like Abraham, and one of the benefits is being God's friend.

Often, God will use a simple truth to reveal a divine truth. Here's what He showed me.

My mother is my best friend. We have a precious relationship that is solid. We laugh, cry, shop, and get lost on the interstate together. In addition to being my parent, she is also my friend. That fact, however, does not diminish her place in my life, one that requires respect. Honoring her role as parent allows me to enjoy her role as friend.

As a child, I saw her only as my mother. But as I matured and became an adult, she could also be my friend. The same thing applies to our relationship with God. We can experience His sovereignty, His authority, *and* His friendship.

One phone call led this sojourner on a detour, allowing her to learn something profound: God wants to be our friend.

TRAVEL DIARY

What is your personal definition of a friend?

_____

_____

_____

Do some of the words in your personal definition also reflect some of the characteristics of God? _____

Which ones? _____

_____

_____

The Merriam-Webster's dictionary defines *friend* as:

1. "One attached to another by affection or esteem.

2. One that is not hostile; one that is of the same nation, party or group.

3. One that favors or promotes something (as a charity).

4. A favored companion."

Based on the above definition, do you think you are ready to include friend on the list of other roles God plays in your life? _____

Why or why not?_____

_____

When we compare the following scriptures with the dictionary, we can see that God does fill that description of friend to us.

1. One attached to another by affection or esteem.

   The LORD appeared to us in the past, saying: "I have loved you with an everlasting love; I have drawn you with loving-kindness." (Jeremiah 31:3 NIV)

2. One that is not hostile; one that is of the same nation, party or group.

   Who shall separate us from the love of Christ? Shall trouble or hardship or persecution or famine or nakedness or danger or sword. (Romans 8:35 NIV)

Since we are of His kingdom, we are in a nation of believers.

   I will walk among you and will be your God and you will be my people. (Leviticus 26:12 NIV)

3. One that favors or promotes.

   And the LORD said to Joshua, "Today I will begin to exalt you in the eyes of all Israel, so that they may know that I am with you as I was with Moses." (Joshua 3:7 NIV)

4. A favored companion.

   But you, O Israel, my servant, Jacob whom I have chosen, you descendants of Abraham my friend. (Isaiah 41:8 NIV)

Which of the following describes your present relationship with God?

_____intimate and close_____somewhat close_____God seems distant

Are there any roadblocks preventing you from getting back on the main road to enjoying your relationship with God? Briefly describe them here.

Roadblocks to a friendship with God can include:

- *Lack of time.* A true friendship requires time. Is time with the Lord a priority for you?_____

- *Attitude.* Is your attitude toward God open and loving?_____

- *Perception.* Satan, our enemy, would like us to think we are unworthy to be a friend of God. However, God's Word says otherwise. Who are you going to believe?

Are you ready to think of the sovereign Lord as your friend? If not, don't rush it. God has a remarkable timetable. Wait for Him.

TRAVELING MERCIES

Dear Lord,
To think that You would call me friend is amazing. I am humbled and honored. Please help me to live my life worthy of our friendship—loyal, committed, trustworthy, and loving. Amen.

(For an amazing song about friendship with God, search the Internet for Travis Cottrell's version of "Friend of God." It will bless your heart!)

SNAPSHOT

"And the Scripture was fulfilled that says, 'Abraham believed God, and it was credited to him as righteousness,' and he was called God's friend." (James 2:23 NIV)

A Relationship with God

If you've not had an opportunity to invite Jesus Christ into your life, now is the perfect time. It's very simple but life changing. If you have then you might want to hold on to this simple plan to share with a friend later.

1. Understand that you are loved.

   For God so loved the world that he gave his one and only Son, that whoever believes in him shall not perish but have eternal life. (John 3:16 NIV)

2. Recognize that all people fall short.

   For all have sinned and fall short of the glory of God. (Romans 3:23 NIV)

3. Respond by turning from sin.

   Repent, then, and turn to God, so that your sins may be wiped out, that times of refreshing may come from the Lord. (Acts 3:19 NIV)

4. Place your faith in Christ as Savior and Lord.

   That if you confess with your mouth, "Jesus is Lord," and believe in your heart that God raised Him from the dead, you will be saved. For everyone who calls on the name of the Lord will be saved. (Romans 10:9, 13 NIV)

5. Pray for salvation.

   "Lord Jesus, I confess that I am a sinner. I believe you died for my sins and that God raised you from the dead. I repent of my sin. I ask you to forgive me and to save me from my sin. Thank you for saving me and giving me eternal life. Help me as I begin this new life. Amen."

WEEK 1, DAY 2
TRAVELING COMPANIONS: ELIZABETH & MARY

SIGHTSEEING

Before I leave on a road trip, I like to know a little bit about the place where I am going and the people I will be traveling with. So, before we begin, allow me to prepare you for our trip and to briefly introduce you to our traveling companions: Elizabeth, and Mary. Like many of your relationships, Elizabeth and Mary shared a history together. Let's take a brief look at theirs.

Our journey does not begin during an exciting time in history, but a time when God's chosen people were desperate for evidence that He existed. Have you ever been in a place like that? Have you ever been desperate for God? Me too.

Since Elizabeth and Mary lived in this culture, they understood what desperation meant. They were desperate for a redeemer. However, neither of them had any idea that they would play an essential role in God's plan to answer the prayers of His people.

For us to truly grasp what remarkable women they were, we will travel back to the times in which they lived and even before. Whether you are a long-time student of the Word, or just beginning, this might be unfamiliar territory. Scripture is full of adventures, so brace yourself as we embark to one of the darkest times in history. Just remember the "light is on the way!"

An Unusual Time—The History

The time span from the end of the book of Malachi, until the beginning of the Gospel of Matthew is 400 years. These are referred to as the inter-testamental years, or the silent years of God. Our road trip begins here.

Imagine this: for 400 years, God did not speak!

It had not always been that way. From the beginning, God always desired a relationship with man—one that included communication. What an awesome thought! God created us in His image and with the ability to communicate with Him!

Today we are fortunate to have numerous versions of the Bible available along with the power of the Holy Spirit dwelling in us. We can communicate with God at any moment. But during the Old Testament times, God spoke to His chosen people (the nation of Israel) through His prophets. Beginning with Moses and right on through Malachi, God's people would gather and hear, "Hear ye O Israel, thus saith the Lord." Then the prophet would deliver a fresh word from God. God was communicating. What set Israel apart from other nations was the fact that God spoke to them. Israel was God's chosen people, set apart to be a priestly nation and an example to the rest of the world. Other nations had hundreds of gods, but Israel's God was alive and communicated with them.

As long as the lines of communication remain open, a relationship exists, but once communication stops, the relationship ends. That is what happened with Israel.

Think for a moment of a past relationship that has now ended, perhaps due to a disagreement, relocation, or a change in the life of one or more people. As you think back, can you pinpoint a time when regular communication with that person stopped?

Lasting and healthy relationships require good communication. As believers, we are His chosen people and we too are set apart as an example to others. To fulfill this blessed call, communication with God is essential.

Knowing that God is a loving God who desires intimacy, I had to ask myself, "What happened?" Why would God stop communicating with His chosen people for so long? I didn't have to look far to find the answer. It was never God's desire to end communication with His people…it was theirs.

The following verses provide insights into what happened.

> They say to the seers, "See no more visions!" and to the prophets, "Give us no more visions of what is right! Tell us pleasant things, prophecy illusions. Leave this way, get off this path, and stop confronting us with the Holy One of Israel!" (Isaiah 30:10-11 NIV)

These were God's *chosen* people making these statements responding to the prophet! They didn't like the message. They wanted to hear pleasant things. Is that happening in our world today? In our churches? Ponder that thought for a moment.

Now look at Zechariah 7:11-12 NIV.

> But they refused to pay attention; stubbornly they turned their backs and stopped up their ears. They made their hearts as hard as flint and would not listen to the law or to the words that the Lord Almighty had

sent by his Spirit through the earlier prophets. So the LORD Almighty was very angry.

And Zechariah 7:13 NIV:

When I called, they did not listen; so when they called, I would not listen," says the LORD Almighty.

The Lord was angry. And God departed from them, and stopped talking. He gave the people what they requested...silence!

Beloved, we must never allow ourselves to come to a place where God departs from us and stops talking. We never want to experience the silence of God!

Here are a few things that happened during those 400 years of silence:

- Jews could not assemble for prayer.
- Observance of the Sabbath was forbidden.
- Possession of the Scriptures was illegal.
- Circumcision was illegal.
- It was illegal not to participate in the monthly sacrifice honoring Antiochus.
- Death by crucifixion began.

None of this surprised God. Long before these dark days of history began, God had warned His chosen people that there would come a time when there would be a famine—not of food, but of hearing His Word.

"The days are coming," declares the Sovereign LORD, "'when I will send a famine through the land—not a famine of food or a thirst for water, but a famine of hearing the words of the LORD." (Amos 8:11 NIV)

That's where our study begins. His faithful have gathered outside the temple, hungry to hear from Him. They had no idea that today God would finally break His silence.

An old priest, a woman past child-bearing years, and a young virgin would play a major role in God's redemption of the world.

CONVERSATIONS

What amazed you most about the scriptures you read today?

_____

_____

_____

Why do you think it is so hard for people to accept that God has a standard of conduct for His chosen ones? _____

_____

_____

It is essential to understand that the laws of God were given to us for protection. Sin is what separates us from God. If we separate ourselves from God, then we lose communication with Him.

Do you wonder if some in the Body of Christ have stopped up their ears and turned their backs on God? Write your thoughts about this below.

_____

_____

_____

My prayer is that we will never turn our backs or close our ears to God's Word. When God convicts us, it is only to redeem us.

How is your communication with God? Check all that apply.

_____Great! I am in His Word and pray daily.

_____I enjoy reading God's Word. It is a love letter to me and a road map for life.

————I pray at church and when I have special needs.

————I don't pray often because I'm unsure if God really listens or if it really matters.

————I don't have as much time as I would like but I read some Scripture during the week.

———— I get enough just from attending church.

We've covered some difficult miles today, but there is one thing that we must hold onto. Communicating with God and others is essential in building lasting relationships.

Girlfriends, start today. Talk to your heavenly Father, enjoy His word, and listen—He has good news for you!

 TRAVEL DIARY

Take a moment to record a prayer in your journal, asking God to make you aware of how important communicating with Him is. Ask Him to help you build this skill throughout this study.

Communication with God begins in His Word. Jeremiah 33:3 NIV says, "Call to me and I will answer you and tell you great and unsearchable things you do not know." Our part is to call to Him; His promise is that He will answer.

TRAVELING MERCIES

Father,
I want to communicate with You, and I know that
communication includes listening. I surrender to
You today. Help me to hear Your voice. Amen.

SNAPSHOT

Knowing the Bible is one thing, knowing the author is another.

Week 1, Day 3
Journaling with Jesus—The Travel Diary

 ### Sightseeing

Since our journey is going to be so exciting, I recommend that along with your Bible and this study guide, you purchase a journal to record your thoughts. Journals are inexpensive, but once they become filled with praise and prayers, they become priceless. For this particular study you may want to buy a pretty journal or notebook, but whatever your choice, get one that will be a joy to use. You can even use your computer if you like! It does not matter what you write in—it matters that you write it down.

If you are already in the habit of journaling, you know the benefits it provides. If not, give it a try. It will be a wonderful opportunity for you to experience the Scriptures in a new way.

Conversations

Most days when I journal, I essentially write a letter to the Lord letting Him know my thoughts, my concerns and my needs. Journaling helps me to remain focused during my prayer time. Some days, I write pages, and other days, a paragraph. I have been doing this for many years, and it has been a wonderful learning process. I also grew to realize the power in God's Word, so I began to combine scriptures with my prayers. Here is a brief example of one of my entries:

> *Dear God,*
> *How majestic is Your name! I praise You that I am fearfully and wonderfully made in Your image. Since You are my Creator, You know that I am suffering with back pain. I am having difficulty sitting at the computer and traveling. With two speaking engagements this week, it requires both, therefore I pray for Your healing. In Psalm 103:2 NIV, Your Word says, "Praise the Lord, O my soul, and forget not all his benefits—who forgives all your sins and heals all your diseases ..."*
> *That will be my hope today, for my hope is in You.*

I also list my prayer requests, praise reports, and special thoughts that I want to remember.

Now, go get yourself a beautiful journal or notebook. Better yet, call your girlfriends and arrange a "journal jaunt." Go to a stationery or Christian bookstore together, select journals for each other, (try to keep each other from seeing them) then go for lunch or coffee and present your gifts to each other!

As you write in your own journal, do not feel that you have to fill up the page. Let the Lord guide you. You will be amazed when you go back a year later and read your journal. It will be evidence that God was, and is, working in your life.

Travel Diary

God knew the importance of remembering what He was doing. He established celebrations, feasts, and memorial practices with His children. In Scripture we find Him instructing His people to write! Look up the following verses and copy them down in your journal.

Exodus 17:14 _____

_____

_____

Exodus 34:27 _____

_____

_____

Deuteronomy 11:20 _____

_____

_____

Proverbs 3:3 _____

_____

_____

Revelation 21:15 _____

_____

_____

Now doesn't that make you want to journal?

 TRAVELING MERCIES

Father,
As I write down elements of this new journey, help me to see Your faithfulness,
Your guidance, and Your love. I want to grow deeper in my relationship with
You. Amen.

 SNAPSHOT

"People who keep journals have life twice" (Jessamyn West). American
Author

WEEK 1, DAY 4
DON'T FORGET THE MAP

 ### SIGHTSEEING

I have never been one who could read a road map. In fact, I owe a debt of gratitude to the dear souls who created Mapquest ™ and the GPS tracking system. Hopefully there will be stars in their crowns for their efforts. My years of traveling in ministry have taught me one sure thing—to get where I need to go, I must have a map. The same is true of this journey. Our map is God's Word.

If you are new to studying Scripture, it can seem overwhelming. I know exactly how you feel.

My grandfather was the major male influence in my life. A hard working professional, he loved his family and his Lord passionately. He also had a yearning for Scripture. His leisure time found him with a Bible in one hand and a commentary in the other. He was a brilliant man who could explain and memorize scriptures with ease.

I inherited his love for the Word, but not his intellectual or natural ability to comprehend and memorize scriptures. So, I have to work very hard to understand. Yet, I am living proof that diligence, commitment, and the power of the Holy Spirit will help you understand God's Word in ways that escape the imagination.

Should you struggle with comprehension, remember that it has nothing to do with our love of God. His Word is for all of us. Most of the men who wrote the Scriptures were simple learners.

Throughout this study, for your convenience, I have provided many of the scriptures already written out so that you will not have to look them up. However, I hope you will, and to encourage that, I have purposely not written out all of them. Reading the scripture from your very own Bible will have a personal impact. Simply reading the Word doesn't change us, but studying the Word does. Webster defines "study" as "diligence, applying the mind, consider attentively, examine closely." Don't be afraid to underline, highlight, or jot personal notes or prayers in your copy of God's Word as you study each verse and passage.

Tips for Studying God's Word

1. Approach the Scriptures with a reverent attitude.

2. Read slowly and with intent—learn to *need* God's Word.

3. Read with the intent of teaching it to someone else.

4. Read only a few scriptures at a time.

5. Read the scripture in more than one version. This may help your understanding.

6. When you do not understand a passage, ask the Lord for help.

7. Accept that there are many scriptures that we may never understand completely.

8. Always begin and end with prayer. Ask God how you can apply the verses or passage immediately.

 ## Conversations

With each lesson that follows, I have prayed diligently that I would maintain reverence for God's Word and interpret it accurately. Throughout the study I will share my own interpretation combined with some of the most knowledgeable biblical scholars in history. I'm praying that you will discover that God's Word is alive and applicable to you.

Looking back, I realized that while my grandfather had a divine gift to understand Scripture, he also proved himself to be a devoted and diligent student of the Word. May the same be said of us, fellow travelers.

The following page contains the main scripture for our study. You will read it often in the coming days. Today we will read Luke 1-25.

Our Scripture for the Journey:

Luke 1:1-56 NIV:
> Many have undertaken to draw up an account of the things that have been fulfilled among us, just as they were handed down to us by those who from the first were eyewitnesses and servants of the word. Therefore, since I myself have carefully investigated everything from the beginning, it seemed good also to me to write an orderly account for you, most

excellent Theophilus, so that you may know the certainty of the things you have been taught.

In the time of Herod king of Judea there was a priest named Zechariah, who belonged to the priestly division of Abijah; his wife Elizabeth was also a descendant of Aaron. Both of them were upright in the sight of God, observing all the Lord's commandments and regulations blamelessly. But they had no children, because Elizabeth was barren; and they were both well along in years.

Once when Zechariah's division was on duty and he was serving as priest before God, he was chosen by lot, according to the custom of the priesthood, to go into the temple of the Lord and burn incense. And when the time for the burning of incense came, all the assembled worshipers were praying outside.

Then an angel of the Lord appeared to him, standing at the right side of the altar of incense. When Zechariah saw him, he was startled and was gripped with fear. But the angel said to him: "Do not be afraid, Zechariah; your prayer has been heard. Your wife Elizabeth will bear you a son, and you are to give him the name John. He will be a joy and delight to you, and many will rejoice because of his birth, for he will be great in the sight of the Lord. He is never to take wine or other fermented drink, and he will be filled with the Holy Spirit even from birth. Many of the people of Israel will he bring back to the Lord their God. And he will go on before the Lord, in the spirit and power of Elijah, to turn the hearts of the fathers to their children and the disobedient to the wisdom of the righteous—to make ready a people prepared for the Lord."

Zechariah asked the angel, "How can I be sure of this? I am an old man and my wife is well along in years."

The angel answered, "I am Gabriel. I stand in the presence of God, and I have been sent to speak to you and to tell you this good news. And now you will be silent and not able to speak until the day this happens, because you did not believe my words, which will come true at their proper time."

Meanwhile, the people were waiting for Zechariah and wondering why he stayed so long in the temple. When he came out, he could not speak to them. They realized he had seen a vision in the temple, for he kept making signs to them but remained unable to speak.

When his time of service was completed, he returned home. After this his wife Elizabeth became pregnant and for five months remained in seclusion. "The Lord has done this for me," she said. "In these days he has shown his favor and taken away my disgrace among the people."

In the sixth month, God sent the angel Gabriel to Nazareth, a town in Galilee, to a virgin pledged to be married to a man named Joseph, a descendant of David. The virgin's name was Mary. The angel went to her and said, "Greetings, you who are highly favored! The Lord is with you."

Mary was greatly troubled at his words and wondered what kind of greeting this might be. But the angel said to her, "Do not be afraid, Mary, you have found favor with God. You will be with child and give birth to a son, and you are to give him the name Jesus. He will be great and will be called the Son of the Most High. The Lord God will give him the throne of his father David, and he will reign over the house of Jacob forever; his kingdom will never end."

"How will this be," Mary asked the angel, "since I am a virgin?"

The angel answered, "The Holy Spirit will come upon you, and the power of the Most High will overshadow you. So the holy one to be born will be called the Son of God. Even Elizabeth your relative is going to have a child in her old age, and she who was said to be barren is in her sixth month. For nothing is impossible with God."

"I am the Lord's servant," Mary answered. "May it be to me as you have said." Then the angel left her.

At that time Mary got ready and hurried to a town in the hill country of Judea, where she entered Zechariah's home and greeted Elizabeth. When Elizabeth heard Mary's greeting, the baby leaped in her womb, and Elizabeth was filled with the Holy Spirit. In a loud voice she exclaimed: "Blessed are you among women, and blessed is the child you will bear! But why am I so favored, that the mother of my Lord should come to me? As soon as the sound of your greeting reached my ears, the baby in my womb leaped for joy. Blessed is she who has believed that what the Lord has said to her will be accomplished!"

And Mary said: "My soul glorifies the Lord and my spirit rejoices in God my Savior, for he has been mindful of the humble state of his servant.

From now on all generations will call me blessed, for the Mighty One has done great things for me—holy is his name.

His mercy extends to those who fear him, from generation to generation.

He has performed mighty deeds with his arm; he has scattered those who are proud in their inmost thoughts. He has brought down rulers from their thrones but has lifted up the humble. He has filled the hungry with good things but has sent the rich away empty. He has helped his servant Israel, remembering to be merciful to Abraham and his descendants forever, even as he said to our fathers."

Mary stayed with Elizabeth for about three months and then returned home.

When it was time for Elizabeth to have her baby, she gave birth to a son. Her neighbors and relatives heard that the Lord had shown her great mercy, and they shared her joy.

 ## TRAVEL DIARY

As you read through the passage above, what were your first thoughts?

_____

_____

_____

How do you picture Gabriel?

_____

_____

_____

Jot down your thoughts concerning Zachariah.

_____

_____

_____

What initial thoughts do you have about Elizabeth?

_____

_____

_____

Why did Luke write his gospel for us? (vs. 3-4)

_____

_____

_____

TRAVELING MERCIES

Father,
Thank You for providing Scripture to me so that I can learn about Your
story! I pray that You will open my heart to what You want me to learn
through this visit with Elizabeth and Mary. Amen.

SNAPSHOT

"All Scripture is God-breathed and is useful for teaching, rebuking, correcting and training in righteousness, so that the man of God may be thoroughly equipped for every good work" (2 Timothy 3:16-17 NIV).

Women of Incredible Faith

N ow that our bags are packed, we are ready to travel down the Freeway of Faith! We have many miles to cover and much to learn. I am thrilled to be your tour guide and traveling companion.

This week we will set our hearts on learning how to become women of incredible faith, women who not only believe *in* God, but also *believe* God. Incredible means "so extraordinary as to seem impossible," and we will see this in action!

God has provided a marvelous role model for us—an elderly woman named Elizabeth who received an answer to a prayer that began in her youth. In addition to her miraculous pregnancy, she would be one of the first to know that the Messiah was coming, and the woman to mentor the mother of God's Son. This calling would require incredible faith.

To follow her example, we too must be women of incredible faith as we prepare for the Second Coming of Christ.

Itinerary

Day 1—A Bout with Doubt

Day 2—More Than We Can Imagine!

Day 3—A Woman of Faith

Day 4—Faithful When We Don't Understand

✦ Travel Tip

"Now faith is being sure of what we hope for and certain of what we do not see." (Hebrews 11:1 NIV)

WEEK 2, DAY 1
A BOUT WITH DOUBT

SIGHTSEEING

In our introductory lesson, we discussed a time in history, long before the earthly life, death, and resurrection of Christ, when God was silent. As believers we have God's promise that He will never leave us or forsake us (Hebrews 13:5). Yet sometimes in our personal journey of faith, we feel as though He has left us. Even though we have received Christ as our personal Savior and have the indwelling of the Holy Spirit, sometimes we hit a roadblock and God seems silent.

When overwhelming hardships and heartache occur, and God doesn't answer quickly or provide answers, there is a sense of rejection. Sometimes we doubt. We wonder, "If God is really who He says He is, then where is He?" We pray. We search the Scriptures. We sit faithfully in our church seats, but God remains silent.

We are not the only ones who have felt this way. In Jeremiah 12, the "weeping prophet" complained to the Lord, saying in effect, "Lord, I know You are righteous, but I don't understand why You are allowing these heartbreaks." I would venture to say that many of us who have had a long history with God have expressed these very same words.

In his book *When God Doesn't Make Sense*, Dr. James Dobson, founder of Focus on the Family, describes it as "feeling abandoned by God." I never heard a better description, because I have felt exactly like that at certain times in my life.

I remember vividly one specific time when God was silent.

I had been a dance teacher and choreographer. I loved my work. It was my life. Then one day, while working in my studio, I twisted my knee. The injury was so severe that I could no longer teach or dance full time. I was devastated to say the least.

In addition to the heartache of not being able to dance, I agonized over what I would do for the rest of my life. I had been such an active person and had worked on exciting projects with professionals from across the country. The void in my life was so huge only God could fill it. I camped in the Scriptures, stayed on my knees, and God seemed to stay where He was…far away. The journey was long before I found the answer.

I had no idea that He was working on something far greater than I could imagine. He was building a new future for me. To do the work He was calling me to do, He needed a woman who would seek Him with all of her heart—a woman who would not easily give up in pursuit of her heavenly Father. He simply wanted me to trust His Word. As I now look back on that time, I remember a valuable lesson:

Feelings are not fact. They are emotions which constantly change.

God's Word says, "… 'Never will I leave you, never will I forsake you'" (Hebrews 13:5 NIV). It does *not* say, "You will always *feel* my presence." Just because I couldn't sense or feel God's presence did not mean He had forsaken me. It is like having a close relationship with a dear friend who lives in another area. Just because you do not experience her physical presence does not mean the relationship is forsaken. God's Word says He will be with you always. Do you believe that?

One of the most common mistakes we make as believers is to seek an *experience* rather than to seek God. While God desires that we sense His presence, He is far more concerned that we trust Him.

CONVERSATIONS

Throughout my relationship with God, there have been times when I have ached to hear from Him, and He remained silent. How about you? Do you recall a time during your faith journey when you felt as though God were silent? If yes, briefly describe that experience here:

What emotions did you experience?

_____ loneliness

_____ hurt

_____ disappointment

_____ depression

_____ frustration

How did you deal with your emotions? _____

_____

_____

_____ spent more time in prayer

_____ spent more time in scripture

_____ stayed busy at church

_____ talked to friends

_____ became angry with God

_____ withdrew

_____ other _____

Often God desires that we seek Him with everything we have, not for His benefit, but for ours. In our search to know His will, we discover things that we would never know otherwise. God's desire is that we keep searching until we realize that He is all we need.

If you are at a place where God seems silent and you feel forgotten, please remember that while you can't always see His hand, you can always trust His Word. He is at work! Romans 8:28 says, "And we know that in all things God works for the good of those who love him, who have been called according to his purpose" (NIV).

If the greatest "heroes of faith" experienced bouts with doubt, we should not be surprised that we will too! Our goal is to overcome our doubt with faith. You are going to study the life of a woman who had unwavering faith. First, let's pull over from our road trip, and take a few moments to examine our own faith.

TRAVEL DIARY

Stop for a moment and evaluate where you are in your faith journey.

Do I believe God, or simply believe that He exists?

_____

_____

_____

Do I believe that God can do what He says He can do?

_____ Why? _____

_____

_____

Do I trust God with everything: my finances, _____ my family _____ my future _____ ? If not then what's holding me back?

_____

What are some ways that I demonstrate my faith?

_____

_____

_____

Do I believe that God's Word is the absolute truth? _____

Is my faith pleasing to God? _____

 ## TRAVELING MERCIES

Dear Father,
In Your Word, You say that without faith it is impossible to please You
(Hebrews 11:6). Father, help me develop a strong faith. Help me trust
Your Word and believe it. Father, I want to seek You, not a feeling or
experience. Help my unbelief, Father, and make me into a mighty
woman of faith. Amen.

 ## SNAPSHOT

To strengthen others, our own faith must be strong.

WEEK 2, DAY 2
MORE THAN WE CAN IMAGINE!—FAITHFUL FRIENDS

SIGHTSEEING

The Scripture for today is Luke 1:5-25.

I can hardly wait for you to open your Bible and begin reading. Today you will meet one of my favorite people and your traveling companion Elizabeth. Her story is shared only in the Gospel of Luke, and it is powerful! Often we read it during the Christmas season, but I am praying that you will experience our Scripture with a tender heart of:

- Compassion over the disappointment of a childless couple

- Respect and admiration for Elizabeth's unwavering faith

- Elation when she discovers that God has much bigger dreams for her.

So girlfriend, take your time, enjoy the Scriptures, remembering the depressing times in which she lived.

The Perfect Couple

In the midst of these harsh times being experienced by the Jewish people, Luke introduces us to a faithful couple—an elderly priest named Zechariah and his wife Elizabeth. Many scholars believe that Zechariah and Elizabeth were in their eighties, based on Zechariah's statement, "I am an old man and my wife is well along in years" (Luke 1:18 NIV).

Both Elizabeth and her husband were descendants of the tribe of Aaron. No families in the world were more honored by God than those of Aaron and David. One was part of the covenant of the priesthood; the other, royalty.

I can only imagine the moment Zechariah knew that Elizabeth was the one for him. Since they were from the same tribe, they likely knew each other from youth. I believe God favored Zechariah's heart in such a way that he was smitten with Elizabeth. Before the foundations of the earth were formed, God had chosen this couple to be parents of John the Baptist—something they never could have imagined! When these two married, there was much rejoicing. A priest had married the daughter of a priest, keeping the dignity of the priesthood according to the laws of Moses.

Like all married couples, they entered marriage with big dreams and expectations. Their dream was to have children—many children. However, Elizabeth was barren.

To grasp how devastating this was for her, we must understand that in those days, a woman lived for one purpose: to have children. To a Jewish woman, nothing was more fundamental than having children. Nothing was worse than a Jewish woman who could not have children. Women who were barren were shamed and humiliated by their communities and were the source of constant gossip. Many believed that God had closed Elizabeth's womb because of some sin. Perhaps the reason Luke establishes the couple's piety from the beginning is to allow readers to know that Elizabeth's barrenness was not due to punishment from God, but was instead meant to further the purposes of God. It wasn't just the stigma that burdened Elizabeth; it was the heartache of not being a mother, or providing an heir for Zechariah. Each month began with hope and ended with heartache.

CONVERSATIONS

As I studied the culture in which Elizabeth lived, I wondered if she had a special woman friend with whom to share her heartache—someone who would not condemn or judge her. Did she have a compassionate friend with a listening ear like the one described in the following verse?

> Praise be to the God and Father of our Lord Jesus Christ, the Father of compassion and the God of all comfort, who comforts us in all our troubles, so that we can comfort those in any trouble with the comfort we ourselves have received from God (2 Corinthians 1:3-4 NIV).

Did she have a friend who strongly believed in God's faithfulness because sometimes the "impossible dream" comes true? Then I had to ask myself the hard question. Would I have been that kind of friend to Elizabeth? If God's answer was no, could I help her to believe that He still loved her? I pray that we can be that kind of friend to the women God places in our circle of influence. God desires for us to be a friend who stays the course and continues to pray for the "impossible dream" to become reality. With God, dreams often come true. Elizabeth is living proof of that! In her wildest dreams she could never have imagined the bigger dream God had for her. Neither can we.

At this stage of her life, Elizabeth had resigned herself to the fact that she would never see her dream turn into reality. Then, her husband returned from his temple service, and nothing could have prepared her for what was about to happen in her life. God had a much bigger dream for Elizabeth. She would be a mother and provide an heir for Zechariah. Her son would be the forerunner to the Messiah!

God's answer to Elizabeth's dream hadn't been no…it was…just wait!

Look at Luke 1:14-17, and list the words that Gabriel uses to describe Elizabeth's son:

He will be…(Fill in the blank.)

_____   _____   _____

_____   _____   _____

_____   _____   _____

God even named her son!

Travel Diary

When my dance career ended, I had no idea that God, the Dream Maker, had a *new* dream waiting for me—you!

Have you ever had a dream, a desire that meant everything to you, that did not become reality? _____

_____

_____

Were you able to make peace with God over the disappointment?

_____

_____

_____

Do you believe that God loves you and has a plan for your life?

_____ Share your thoughts

_____

_____

_____

Are still waiting on a dream? _____ What are you doing to make

it happen? _____

_____

_____

_____

If that dream has ended, do you have a new dream?
Briefly write your thoughts here.

_____

_____

_____

Do you have special friends to encourage you? Give them a call or e-mail them
for a chat of encouragement.

If you have lost your hope and feel as if you have gone past the age of
"dreaming," meditate on these two verses from the apostle Paul. Write them in
your journal along with your thoughts and prayer surrounding them.

> Now to Him who is able to do immeasurably more than all we ask or
> imagine, according to His power that is at work within us…(Ephesians
> 3:20 NIV)

> No eye has seen, no ear has heard, no mind has conceived what God has
> prepared for those who love him. (1 Corinthians 2:9 NIV)

I don't know what your dream is. However, I know God does not put an age limit on dreams! You are never too young or too old to follow God's dream.

Do you have a dream? What has kept you from going after your dream? Money? Time? Attitude? Let me encourage you to follow your dream. Write that book. Take that class. Dance that dance. Please invite God, the Dream Maker, to be involved every step of the way. It will become much more than you can imagine, so dream on, girlfriend!

TRAVELING MERCIES

Dear Father,
Help me to become a woman who realizes that Your dream is much bigger than anything I could imagine and to wait patiently on You. Lord, I also ask that You help me to be faithful to those women in my life who are an "Elizabeth" and are hurting. Help me to be compassionate, a good listener, and a faithful friend who demonstrates Your faithfulness. Amen.

SNAPSHOT

When God is getting ready to do a mighty work in our lives, age is never a factor.

TRAVEL TIP

One book I'd like to recommend if you need encouragement to dream again: *When a Woman Discovers Her Dream,* by Cindi McMenamin.

WEEK 2, DAY 3
A WOMAN OF FAITH

SIGHTSEEING

From the moment I began my in-depth study on Elizabeth, it was obvious that I was meeting a woman of unwavering faith. I found that to be amazing considering the culture in which she lived and the difficulties she endured. Five hundred years had gone by without any miracles or visible evidence from God. These were desperate times for the nation of Israel.

The only thing that would redeem and reconcile Israel's relationship with God was a Savior. Before Gabriel's visit Elizabeth had no idea that the Messiah was on His way, and that *she* would be involved in this history-defining moment. In fact, this elderly woman of unwavering faith was one of the first to know and prepare for the Messiah's coming.

Like Elizabeth, we live in desperate times. People all around us need a Savior. I believe that we are also living on the edge of a history-defining moment—the Second Coming of the Messiah!

If this is true, then God is looking for "Elizabeths" in the 21st century to prepare the "Marys" of our world for this coming event. To fulfill this calling, we too must be women of unwavering faith.

CONVERSATIONS

How important is faith to God? Hebrews 11:6a NIV tells us: "And without faith it is impossible to please God …" Think about how powerful that scripture is. We can be the best Sunday school teacher, attend every Bible study available, volunteer many hours each week; yet if we lack faith, then we are not pleasing to God.

But what *is* faith? Hebrews 11:1 NIV defines it this way:

> Now faith is being sure of what we hope for and certain of what we do not see.

Simply put, we must *believe* what we cannot *see*. One of the best definitions of faith I have heard is this:

> To a believer faith means that God tells the truth.

There are times we cannot see any evidence of God at work, or feel His presence. These are the very times that we must trust His Word. Jesus said in Matthew 28:20, "…and surely I am with you always, to the very end of the age." We must believe that, even if we are in a season without visible evidence.

Elizabeth's life had not turned out as she had hoped, but she remained faithful. Her faith was based on who God was and His history with His people.

The mark of a true woman of faith is that she will serve God in spite of difficulties and unexplainable heartache. During my ministry, I have met women who have suffered heartache so tragic that I stand in awe of their faithfulness. I wonder if I would do the same. These women are my heroes! I have witnessed their unwavering faith in spite of great loss. To me there is no greater witness for Christ or better testimony of faith.

How do they do it?

My heroes of faith made a choice. They chose to take God's hand and allow Him to lead them *through* the valley. They accepted that "valley days" were part of life and the best way *out* was to go *through* with God.

> … He guides me in paths of righteousness for his name's sake. Even though I walk through the valley of the shadow of death, I will fear no evil, for you are with me. Your rod and your staff, they comfort me. (Psalm 23:3-4 NIV)

God never meant for us to dwell in the valley alone, but to draw closer to Him.

Read Psalm 32:7-8 and write it out below. This is a good verse to memorize and share with others.

_____

_____

_____

God is with us. He will lead us in the direction that we should go. These are essential truths that women in our lives need to know. As women of faith we can share our personal heartaches, those times when we didn't think we could put one foot in front of the other, but God reached down, took our hands, and walked with us. By sharing our experiences, we have the opportunity to help other women through their valley days. We may even help them avoid some valley days completely! As difficult as some of them have been, isn't it wonderful that with God's redeeming love we can use these experiences to help others?

Elizabeth's "valley days" enabled her to be the prefect mentor for Mary the mother of the Messiah.

 TRAVEL DIARY

Based on what we have learned about Elizabeth so far, list some of her "valley day" experiences that might be helpful to Mary. (Think of feelings of rejection, disappointment, etc.)

_____

_____

_____

What are some "valley days" that you have experienced that could be helpful to others in their faith journey?

_____

_____

_____

If God has not already done so, someday He will put someone in your life who can learn from and be encouraged by your experience(s). These could include divorce, financial difficulties, loss of a loved one, personal health issues, infertility, parenting challenges, learning difficulties, relocation away from family and friends, loss of income, or unpleasant relationships. Sometimes we are tempted to keep our feelings and past experiences to ourselves. Just remember how much you could encourage someone going through a similar challenge by sharing your story appropriately.

Ask God to help you invest in others by sharing your experiences. Begin by seeking His divine guidance, and remember that His answer may come right away or over a period of time. Be patient. Listen and watch for His promptings.

Ask God for permission about what you should share. For example, I experienced abuse in my past, but before I shared my story, I waited until those involved would not be hurt. I sincerely believe that in the body of Christ, we should be sensitive and cautious about what we share and with whom. Some details just aren't necessary. The key is to help people see how much God helped you.

After much prayer, take your journal and put your thoughts on paper. Think back on the experience and consider:

Was there a particular scripture that encouraged you?
Was there a godly woman who prayed for you?
Did you feel God's presence?
Did you record your thoughts and feelings in a journal? Did that help?
Always remember that God never wastes anything.

 TRAVEL TIP

Keep your story simple, honest, and appropriately confidential. At all costs, do not allow this to become an opportunity that Satan can use for evil. If you are uncomfortable sharing, then it isn't time. Trust God for His timing and peace. When the timing is right, you will be amazed at how your testimony will help others. Girlfriends, keep the faith!

TRAVELING MERCIES

> *Dear Father,*
> *You know my past and the difficulties that I have experienced. Thank you for being there with me and helping me to overcome many challenges. Now with your help I desire to be an encouragement to other women who may be going through something similar. I confess that I am feeling _____ (fill in the blank) about sharing, but I surrender to you. Please guide me with Your Word, wisdom, and peace, showing me when, if, and how I should share my story. Help me live my faith and share it with others to Your glory. Thank You for being Lord of the valley. Amen.*

SNAPSHOT

Faith is like a muscle, if we want a strong one then we must build it.

Week 2, Day 4
Faithful When We Don't Understand

 **Sightseeing**

Elizabeth lived in a culture where her self-worth was completely determined through producing an heir. Unfortunately, this was the one thing she could *not* do. Can you imagine her heartache and disappointment? She saw women with more children than they could possibly manage or feed. She would be happy with just one!

It's extremely hard to continue to serve God while He gives others what we desperately want.

I suffered a miscarriage with my first pregnancy. It was devastating. Many of my friends were expecting, and it was difficult to be excited for them. I was also angry with God. I can only imagine what Elizabeth must have felt.

However, Elizabeth was exceptional. As the years went by and she remained childless, she did a remarkable thing. Instead of becoming bitter, she chose to accept God's decision. I doubt she ever understood His decision, but she did what a woman of faith does. She accepted His answer.

I wonder if the words in Isaiah 55:8-9 (NIV) offered her some comfort:

> For my thoughts are not your thoughts, neither are your ways my ways," declares the Lord. "As the heavens are higher than the earth, so are my ways higher than your ways and my thoughts than your thoughts."

What does that scripture say to you?

_____

_____

_____

Conversations

Have you ever been at a place like that when God's answer was no? _____

Looking back now, do you understand why His answer was no? _____

Sometimes, later in life, God will reveal to us why He said no, but there are times when He doesn't.

I was a young girl of eleven when our home burned the week before Christmas. My mother was a struggling single mom with two children and now had lost her home and many possessions. It was one of the saddest moments of my life. I don't think I will ever completely understand why it happened. As a woman of faith, and looking back, I learned two things: our God is faithful, and people are far more precious than things.

As women of faith, we too must accept that there will be many times when God says no and that He will not always offer an explanation to us. What He does offer is grace.

Elizabeth probably had many unanswered questions and was unsure of why God had said no to her desire to have children. Yet I believe that she accepted God's answer with grace and dignity because Luke points out in chapter one, verse six that both of them were upright in the sight of God, observing all the Lord's commandments and regulations blamelessly.

God knows that bitterness bankrupts our capacity to love. Love is who He is and commands that we be (see 1 John 4:8). We cannot give away what we don't possess. Later when she mentored Mary, the mother of the coming Messiah, it would take unselfish love—the kind of love Paul writes about in 1 Corinthians 13:1-13.

Turn to 1 Corinthians 13:1-13 in your Bible and read it aloud slowly. Think about what the words are saying. It's a powerful passage, isn't it?

This is the kind of love Elizabeth lavished on Mary and the kind of love God has asked us to offer the Marys in our world.

Verse 7 of this passage had a real impact on me. Here's what it says about love: it always *protects*.

God knew that Elizabeth would protect a young virgin who would come knocking on her door very soon.

It always *trusts*. Elizabeth's life demonstrated that she loved God enough to trust Him.

It always *hopes*. Elizabeth's love for God provided hope that the Messiah would come.

It always *perseveres*. She remained faithful even when life turned out differently than she expected.

 **TRAVEL DIARY**

Look back to 1 Corinthians 13:1-13 and please fill in each of the blanks below. Then, prayerfully ask God to help you love like this. If there is a particular area you find especially difficult, tell God about it and ask Him to strengthen you in this area. (For example, "love is patient" can be a real struggle!)

Love is_____

Love is _____

It does not _____ It does not _____

It is not_____ It is not _____

It is not easily_____ It keeps no _____

Love does not delight in _____ but with _____.

Now you understand why it is so important to get rid of any bitterness that resides within your heart. If we accept the call to prepare others for the second coming of Christ, we must love the way the Apostle Paul has instructed. Any hint of bitterness will prevent us from ministering effectively.

My pastor from childhood used to say that "Life's heartaches and situations either make us bitter or better—the difference is the letter 'I.'"

Disappointments come. Life is challenging and so unfair. But if we don't guard our hearts, bitterness can easily take root. Do you have unresolved bitterness buried deep inside your heart? A hurt too disappointing or painful to let go? If so, take time *now* to talk with your heavenly Father. Ask Him to heal your broken heart, remove any residue of bitterness, and strengthen you to forgive. You are His child, and He wants you to be whole!

Beloved, do not allow bitterness to rob one more minute of the joy God has planned for you. Jesus came to set the captives free. Let go and let God free you today!

Traveling Mercies

The Serenity Prayer is a short but very powerful prayer used by 12-step recovery programs. Pray it sincerely as you close today's lesson.

"God, grant me the serenity to accept the things I cannot change, courage to change the things I can, and wisdom to know the difference."

(Dr. Reinhold Neibuhr—Theologian, 1892-1971)

Snapshot

The only difference between "bitter" and "better" is the letter "I."

Women Who Revere God: The High Road

The miles are adding up and the adventure continues as we study the friendship of Elizabeth and Mary. Now that we have increased our faith, we are going to need it as we move ahead.

We're going climbing, friend…to the high calling God has placed on our lives. Our starting place is the heart, where God works privately.

I have invited Him to be our tour guide and traveling companion. With your permission, He will navigate through places that need restoration and renewal. His purpose is to help you reach your destination whole and complete.

Should you get discouraged and want to give up, remember the view at the top is spectacular! So put on the old hiking boots, grab plenty of Living Water, and I'll meet you there!

ITINERARY

Day 1–A Bride to Be: Mary's Story

Day 2–You Go, Girl

Day 3–From Sightseer to Holy Seeker

Day 4–The Best Dressed Lady in Town

TRAVEL TIP

"It is the LORD your God you must follow, and him you must revere. Keep his commands and obey him; serve him and hold fast to him" (Deuteronomy 13:4 NIV).

WEEK 3, DAY 1
A BRIDE-TO-BE: MARY'S STORY

SIGHTSEEING

Today we will travel to an obscure village in Galilee. Our former traveling companion, the angel Gabriel, is back serving as a messenger of God. This time, the recipient of his message is a very young, devout Jewish girl. She will join us for the remainder of our journey.

Our Scripture is probably familiar and perhaps a favorite. Take your time as you read Luke 1:26-38, letting yourself imagine all that took place.

At the time of Gabriel's visit, Mary's life was planned. She was engaged to a carpenter named Joseph. According to Matthew 1:19, he was a "righteous man." They were to live in the village in which he worked, and she would be the mother of his children. It would be a typical and ordinary life—nicely planned.

Then, Gabriel showed up, and life would never be the same.

Have you ever had your life planned and suddenly everything was turned upside down? How did you respond?

Mary's first response was fear. Gabriel's presence alone would be enough to frighten her. I cannot imagine Gabriel as small. I picture this messenger of God as large, powerful, and somewhat intimidating due to his holiness. However, it wasn't only his appearance that frightened her, but his greeting as well. He said, "Greetings, you who are highly favored. The Lord is with you."

Can you imagine the thoughts that went through Mary's mind? No one considered women in her culture to be "highly favored." In fact, parents were often disappointed at the birth of a female child. So how could God find favor with a young girl like her?

The angel Gabriel continues. "Do not be afraid, Mary. You have found favor with God." Then Gabriel shares what will happen.

I picture the stunned adolescent trying to process the information she is receiving. Gabriel's words were familiar to her. Devout Jews were looking for the promised Messiah. Yet she never imagined the fulfillment of the promise would involve her!

Mary's humble response, "How can this be, since I am a virgin?" is not a question born of doubt, but rather in seeking instructions and information. When your plans turn upside down, do you seek instruction from God? Certainly this is a valuable lesson we can learn from Mary.

Let's continue. After explaining that the Holy Spirit will cause Mary to conceive, Gabriel speaks another name in verse 36. It is not the name of Mary's mother or her husband-to-be…it is her elderly relative Elizabeth's! Gabriel shares the wonderful news that Elizabeth is in her sixth month of pregnancy.

Have you ever wondered why Gabriel shared this information with Mary?

Perhaps, Gabriel understood how young and vulnerable Mary was and that her generation had not experienced the power of God. I believe that Gabriel wanted to provide both assurance and evidence that Jehovah God was on the move again! If an elderly relative, long past child-bearing years could conceive, then maybe, what the angel said *was* true!

With great confidence Gabriel says, "Nothing is impossible with God!" I imagine he said this with tenderness and power. He had just delivered the greatest news ever told to a woman. "The Messiah is coming, and *you* will be His mother!"

CONVERSATIONS

I wonder if Gabriel's proclamation that "nothing is impossible with God" became Mary's "life verse" in the days ahead when she gave birth in a manger, when she fled to Egypt with Joseph and her toddler, when her son was run out of town, and later nailed to a cross on Calvary. To survive moments like these, I imagine she repeated those words over and over: "Nothing is impossible with God!"

Do you have special scriptures that have become life verses for you? What are they?

_____

_____

_____

I have several life verses that have sustained me during difficult times. When circumstances seem impossible, I find myself recalling a scripture that provides either comfort or a promise.

To be able to recall such verses, we must be in God's Word regularly. I recommend that you purchase index cards, and as you study God's Word, write favorite scriptures down and commit them to memory.

In verse 38, what was Mary's response after Gabriel gave her the news?

She said, "Be it unto me as you have said." With these words, Mary expressed the kind of faith and obedience that helps us understand why she was the one chosen to be the mother of God's Son. As women of faith, may that be our response as well!

TRAVEL DIARY

Earlier, I asked if there had ever been a time when your life was planned, and suddenly everything was turned upside down. Did you respond with faith or fear? Briefly recall.

_____

_____

_____

Were you able to trust God completely?

_____

_____

_____

Looking back, can you see how God was involved?

_____

_____

_____

What did you learn?

_____

_____

_____

"For nothing is impossible with God" (Luke 1:37 NIV). What does that mean to you personally? Do you truly believe this verse?

_____

_____

_____

Is this a time in your life when you need to put that verse into action? What's the "impossible" you need God to do?

_____

_____

_____

Commit this verse to memory and say it every day during our study.

TRAVELING MERCIES

> *Dear Father,*
> *In Your Word, Psalm 139:16b says that "all the days ordained for me were written in your book before one of them came to be." Father, help me to surrender my plans to You. Help me to truly believe with all of my heart, soul, strength, and mind that nothing is impossible with You! Amen*

SNAPSHOT

If we believe nothing is impossible with God, it will be impossible not to believe Him.

Week 3, Day 2
You Go, Girl!

🖼 Sightseeing

When we ended our session yesterday, Gabriel had just announced to Mary that she would be the mother of God's Son, the highest calling ever bestowed on a woman.

What does a young woman do after receiving news like that? Thank goodness we don't have to wonder! Luke 1:39 NIV says, "At that time Mary got ready and hurried to the town in the hill country …"

Most scholars believe that Mary left immediately to go to Elizabeth's home and that she told no one about the angel's visit. I believe that as well. Had she confided in her parents, I doubt they would have let her go, fearing that something could happen to her. The words "got ready" seem to confirm my thoughts. The Greek word for this phrase is *anistemi,* which means "to stand again, to rise up." This means that Mary rose up and departed.

With all of my heart, I believe that Mary was overwhelmed by what took place with Gabriel. As suddenly as the angel appeared he was gone, leaving her alone and amazed. Certainly she must have had many questions. For now, though, she had one mission—to get to Elizabeth.

This would not be a quick or easy trip. Elizabeth lived 90 miles away, which would require three to five days of travel. That would give Mary a long time to ponder the angel's message. I wonder how many times she replayed Gabriel's words in her mind.

Neither fear nor distance would prevent Mary from going to Elizabeth. She knew this was God-ordained. Everything in her life had been thoroughly planned, even the provision of someone with whom to share the experience. How it must have calmed her soul to know that God had provided Elizabeth to help her prepare for this divine calling!

God knew Mary's future and it would be difficult. He understood her need for a very special kind of mentor, someone like herself who was also expecting a miracle child. God's choice for the woman who would mentor the mother of His Son was Elizabeth, and she was ready for the task. In fact, her life had been a preparation for this calling.

Elizabeth had a history with God. From early childhood, she was a woman who revered God and faithfully followed His commandments. In spite of heartache and hard times, she remained faithful. That allowed God to use her greatly.

CONVERSATIONS

Did you know that God can use your history with Him to minister to others? It's true!

You may be thinking, "Me? How could God use someone like me? I'm so ordinary. Besides, you don't know my past." I know. I've been there, said that, and unfortunately, believed it, too.

Neither Elizabeth nor Mary thought they were special either. In fact, Mary refers to her humble state in Luke 1:48 NIV, "for He has been mindful of the humble state of his servant." Elizabeth had an even lower opinion of herself. In Luke 1:25, when she heard that she would be a mother, she said, "The Lord has done this for me," she said. "In these days he has shown his favor and taken away my disgrace among the people." After all these years, the stigma of being barren was still her identity.

Can you relate? I certainly can. I have struggled for most of my life with low self-esteem in spite of many accomplishments. Deep down, I see myself as extremely ordinary and inadequate to share God's Word with audiences around the country. But, praise God, He views me as valuable and useful! God feels the same about you. He knows the plans and purpose He has for you, His beloved daughter.

TRAVEL DIARY

Are there some identity issues or labels from your past branded on your heart?

_____

_____

_____

Beloved, if so, God wants to erase those labels with the words from Ephesians 2:10. Write that verse here and commit it to memory:

_____

_____

_____

The moment we begin a relationship with Christ, we then move forward to the good work that God created us to do! If you find that difficult to accept, then pray and tell God how you feel. Thank Him for creating you and choosing you to be part of His work! Ask Him to show you the unique way He is already using you!

If you sense God calling you to do something special, and you feel inadequate or ordinary, do what Mary did. Get up and make haste to *your* Elizabeth, a godly woman who is faithful, reveres His name, and has a long history with God.

In week six, we will talk further about how to find an Elizabeth. However, if you already know a godly woman that you can trust and feel comfortable with, you go girl! Go right to her doorstep. Talk to her about your feelings of insignificance. Chances are that she's experienced those same feelings herself at some point in her life.

Let's make a pact as sisters in Christ—and girlfriends in God, from this moment on, no matter what our past includes, we will allow God to use it and us for His glory!

TRAVELING MERCIES

Dear Father,
Ephesians 2:10 tells me that I am Your workmanship. You don't make junk! I've been created in Christ Jesus to do good works that You've selected me to do. Sometimes it's hard for me to believe this Lord, but I want to be used by You. Show me where You are already using me, and guide me to the "good works" You have planned. Amen.

SNAPSHOT

When Satan reminds you of your past, remember, he's run out of new material.

WEEK 3, DAY 3
FROM SIGHTSEER TO HOLY SEEKER

SIGHTSEEING

Beloved, I hope you enjoyed our visit to Galilee where we met our new traveling companion, Mary. She will have much to share with us as we travel to Elizabeth's home in Judea.

Our focus this week is to become holy women who revere God. Who better to serve as role models than Elizabeth and Mary? Be prepared: the miles we tread are long and steep. This part of the journey is not really for sightseeing but for *holy seeking*.

In fact, we need God to travel every mile with us today, so let's invite Him to join us:

> *Father, we are seeking to grow more like You in everything we say and do. Help us to know how to do that. Where we are weak, we ask that You provide strength. Where we lack knowledge, we ask that You provide wisdom. Lord, we give You permission to point out areas that need addressing and confessing. We trust You because we are Yours! Amen.*

Godly Women, Ungodly World

In our "cutting-edge" society, I'm not sure we truly understand what "holiness" means. One definition of holy is "set apart for a religious purpose." If we live in holiness, our life is set apart from the philosophy of this world. That way of living will reflect itself in our actions, words, and deeds, and we will imitate the goodness and graciousness of God.

In today's world, it's difficult. We're surrounded by ungodly influences and distractions that offer many temptations. If we are not deliberate and careful to guard our hearts, suddenly we are more like the world than like Christ.

In Romans 12:1-2 NIV, the apostle Paul expresses what believers can do to avoid following this world's standards:

> Therefore, I urge you, brothers, in view of God's mercy, to offer your bodies as living sacrifices, holy and pleasing to God—this is your spiritual

act of worship. Do not conform any longer to the pattern of this world, but be transformed by the renewing of your mind. Then you will be able to test and approve what God's will is—His good, pleasing and perfect will.

The key word in this scripture is *conform*. Let's look at its definition:

1. To be similar or identical; also, to be in agreement or harmony
2. To be obedient or compliant; to act in accordance with prevailing standards or customs.

To conform to this world is to make decisions and live a lifestyle based on current standards and to fit in with its philosophy.

CONVERSATIONS

Think for a moment: are there areas in your life where you have conformed to the world's standards?

Review the following list and prayerfully consider if any of these provide guidance or influence your decisions.

_____Media: movies, television, music

_____ Fashion: clothing, makeup

_____ Material things: homes, vehicles, "stuff"

_____ Reading material: magazines, tabloids, romance novels

_____ Politics: viewpoints on key events and issues

_____ Relationships: approval from your peers, family, workplace

As women seeking to live a holy life, we need to be *very* careful not to put ourselves into compromising situations.

Looking back over Luke 1, what are some obvious ways that Mary and Elizabeth demonstrated a holy lifestyle, one that revered God?

_____   _____   _____

_____   _____   _____

_____   _____   _____

The first things I noticed is their vocabulary—the words they use.

Read Luke 1:42-45. These are the first words Elizabeth speaks the moment Mary steps into her home. Wow!

Now, read Mary's response in Luke 1:46-55. This is known as the Magnificat, which means "to glorify." What are some words she speaks? (Keep in mind how young she was!)

_____   _____

_____   _____

_____   _____

Mary's words provide an in-depth look at her godliness. She quotes 12 different Old Testament passages from 1 Samuel 1-2.

Think about your language—the words you use.

Do your words glorify God and praise His name? _____

Is this something you need to work on? _____

Have you noticed how casually people misuse God's name? _____

Meditate on Deuteronomy 5:11 NIV:

> You shall not misuse the name of the LORD your God, for the LORD your God will not hold anyone guiltless who misuses his name.

Please notice the seriousness of this scripture. God says that He will hold no one guiltless of misusing His name. God's name is above all names. It has the power to heal, to redeem, and to give life and death. Remember that God is looking for people who revere His name, not profane it. How we use God's name will have an impact on our circle of influence.

If you have struggled in this area, I understand. In the world of arts, I was surrounded by people who used profanity habitually. It was easy for me to do the same. However, we serve an amazing God who is ready and able to help us in our areas of weakness. Even one of the greatest prophets in biblical history had the same issue. Let's close our time together by looking at how God delivered him.

TRAVEL DIARY

In closing please read Isaiah 6:1-8. I like to call this "The Encounter."

Standing in the presence of God, there was one area that concerned Isaiah. He was a man of _____ lips. He lived among a people of _____ lips.

We can certainly relate. Everywhere in our world, people use offensive language and words that are inappropriate. If we aren't careful, we become comfortable with this, and soon it no longer offends us.

In verses 6 and 7 we learn what happened to Isaiah.

God sanctified his lips and took away his guilt. Isaiah became one of the greatest prophets in the Old Testament. Those sanctified lips would bring the Holy Word of God to God's people, and Isaiah would become the prophet that Jesus quoted regularly. Think about that! A man delivered by God's grace so that his words would grace the passages of Scripture.

TRAVELING MERCIES

Dear Father,
Sanctify my mouth. May it always be a vessel used for Your glory and never a weapon in Satan's hand. Amen.

SNAPSHOT

From the beginning, God was seeking people who would revere His name. Prayerfully ask yourself …do I?

WEEK 3, DAY 4
THE BEST DRESSED LADY IN TOWN

SIGHTSEEING

I am going to take a guess—perhaps an "educated" one—that for many of you, a road trip includes a shopping trip! I must confess I have never met a mall I didn't like. And I love to shop for clothes! There is a huge interest in fashion in our world. When I did a Google ™ search on fashion consultants, there were over a million listed!

Today, we are going to visit with a top fashion consultant who will provide wardrobe tips that will totally transform us!

Now, I must warn you that this is not your typical consultant from Rodeo Drive in Beverly Hills. Instead, our fashion expert is the apostle Paul and he has some specific instructions for believers who want to be fashion savvy in Christ. As we head over to Colossians, remember that our focus is becoming women who REVERE God, as Mary and Elizabeth did.

CONVERSATIONS

Several years ago, I had the privilege of traveling to the Holy Land. While there, many things had a profound effect on me. The most powerful was my symbolic baptism in the Jordan River. The Jordan is the same river where John the Baptist baptized Jesus. Memorable doesn't even begin to describe that experience.

Before my immersion, the minister asked what I would like the baptism to represent. One word came to mind—holiness. When I came out of the water, I wanted my worldly nature completely gone and washed away.

Since then, I have tried to pursue a life of holiness. Believe me, this requires a determined and deliberate heart, especially in today's world.

However, Elizabeth and Mary also lived in extremely difficult times. With the exception of some devout Jews, they lived among ungodly people who had forsaken God. Yet, they did not. These two women made a choice: they would obey God and live a lifestyle that demonstrated it. God honored them for their obedience.

Let's recall our definition of revere: "to treat and regard Him with admiration and deep respect, to be in awe of, to worship, to honor."

How can we become a living example of that definition? The best place to learn is in God's Word.

Our Scripture reading is Colossians 3:1-17. It is a letter from the apostle Paul, written to the holy and faithful ones in Christ. These verses are packed with "fashion tips" that have the power to transform our mind, body, and soul.

In verse 5, what does Paul say must be put to death?

_____

_____

_____

Paul informs us that because of this lifestyle, the wrath of God is coming. Dear ones, please don't miss that! The wrath of God is something to fear!

In verse 8, list what we must rid ourselves of:

_____

_____

_____

Each spring when we clean out our closets, we get rid of clothing that is no longer in style or doesn't fit appropriately. Paul is telling us that when we become followers of Christ, there are some attitudes and behaviors that no longer fit appropriately either.

Verse 12 gives us the motivation to do this. Write the verse below:

_____

_____

_____

🦶 TRAVEL DIARY

What does being "holy" mean to you personally?

_____

_____

_____

Is being holy a lifestyle? _____

Is it possible to live a holy lifestyle today? _____

Absolutely! If God calls us to do something, be assured He will enable us to do that. His Word is clear—we can do all things through Him! (See Philippians 4:13.)

> But just as he who called you is holy, so be holy in all you do; for it is written: "Be holy, because I am holy." (1 Peter 1:15-16 NIV)

Peter, an old fisherman turned evangelist, wrote those words. After being with Christ, he knew there was only one lifestyle for believers—holiness.

Who determines what holiness is?

_____ my church _____ my culture _____ my community

_____ God's Word

God is the only One who can define holiness; therefore we must look to Him and His Word.

According to Colossians 3:12, God has some specific guidelines concerning our wardrobe choices. Paul has instructed us to clothe ourselves with:

1. _____

2. _____

3. _____

4. _____

5. _____

In verse 14, we surround all these with _____, "which binds them together in perfect _____."

God wants us to make a fashion statement that is quite different from the world, but very "in vogue" with Him. However, we must make the decision to clothe ourselves with these virtues. It won't happen without effort.

As I get dressed each day, my clothes don't magically come out of the closet and onto my body. I have to put on each piece. Girlfriend, if we are going to adopt these fashion strategies, it will take a daily effort on our part. We must do what Paul said—"Set our minds on things above."

These fashion tips, while simple, are very challenging. However, should you apply them regularly, I have no doubt you'll become the "best dressed lady" in God's eyes.

To help this become a daily lifestyle, I suggest you write Colossians 3:12 on an index card. Tape the card somewhere in your closet or on your mirror—someplace where you will see it everyday as you dress, look to the Lord, and pray.

Traveling Mercies

Dear Father,
Here is my new wardrobe. Today, I am putting on compassion, kindness, humility, gentleness, and patience. I ask You to bind them all onto me with love. I want to focus on the beauty that comes from living by Your Word. Amen.

Snapshot

The best fashion tips come from the Word of God.

Women Of Integrity

TRAVEL ADVISORY

This week we are taking the road less traveled—the road called integrity. Sometimes it can be challenging but it is the only way for followers of Christ.

With each mile you travel, believe faithfully that you are getting closer to the "high calling of God." He has exciting plans for you, and He is doing an amazing work in your life.

To reach our destination we will look to our map—God's Word. There are no shortcuts! Becoming a woman of integrity requires the long, steady route. In fact, it is so important to our faith journey that I have added some "bonus miles." So let's get going and see what God has to say.

ITINERARY

Day 1—People of Integrity

Day 2—Secret Keepers

Day 3—Integrity in Marriage

Day 4—Integrity of the Sabbath

Day 5—Bonus Miles: The Friends We Choose

TRAVEL TIP

Do not let this Book of the Law depart from your mouth; meditate on it day and night, so that you may be careful to do everything written in it. Then you will be prosperous and successful (Joshua 1:8 NIV).

WEEK 4, DAY 1
PEOPLE OF INTEGRITY

SIGHTSEEING

As we continue to study the life of Elizabeth and Mary, I believe it will be beneficial for you to know about the Gospel writer who has provided the main text for our study. Interestingly, he is the only Gentile of the four Gospel writers, and the only one to write a sequel (the book of Acts).

If it were not for Luke's gospel, we would not know about:

- The extraordinary couple, Zachariah and Elizabeth

- Gabriel's visit and announcement to Zachariah

- Gabriel's visit and announcement to Mary

- Mary's trip and visit to Elizabeth

- The birth of John the Baptist

Scholars believe that Mary had a close friendship with Luke and that she provided the intimate details that we read in his first two chapters. This would explain how, in addition to the divine inspiration Luke received from God, he was able to share things that only the elderly couple and the young virgin personally experienced.

Luke was a close friend and companion to the apostle Paul. His writing demonstrates that he was a highly educated man, writing from a Greek background and viewpoint.

From the beginning, I sense Luke's passion that his readers know without question that he had thoroughly investigated every word he wrote. His sole purpose was to provide a complete and orderly account of the life of Jesus.

Luke begins his Gospel with the parents of John the Baptist, the forerunner of the Messiah.

Let's read Luke 1:1-3 NIV:

> Many have undertaken to draw up an account of the things that have been fulfilled among us, just as they were handed down to us by those who from the first were eyewitnesses and servants of the word. Therefore,

since I myself have carefully investigated everything from the beginning, it seemed good also to me to write an orderly account for you, most excellent Theophilus.

When studying this text, the word "eyewitness" grabbed my attention. Webster defines eyewitness as "One who himself has seen a specific thing happen." I like knowing that God would include others to witness His work! You will find eyewitnesses throughout Luke's Gospel. I recommend you underline them in your Bible. They will play an important role during our study.

Imagine the Gospel writer thoroughly investigating the background of the parents of John the Baptist. We can only wonder how many witnesses he interviewed. Upon gathering his information, Luke discovers a profound truth about this couple, one so important that he wanted to share it with his readers.

How does Luke 1:6 describe Zachariah and Elizabeth?

They were _____

_____

_____

Who do you think may have served as eyewitnesses for Luke's investigation?

_____

_____

_____

Based on their personal experience, these witnesses could say with assurance that Elizabeth and Zachariah were righteous, observed all the Lord's commands, and were blameless. In other words, they were people of integrity. Let's talk about that.

CONVERSATIONS

To be "blameless" does not mean to be "without sin." If that were true, then Jesus would not have needed to die for us. We are sinners saved by grace, but let's see what Scripture says about being blameless.

In Psalm 19:13, King David says, "Keep your servant also from willful sins; may they not rule over me. Then I will be blameless, innocent of great transgression."

Based on this scripture, what do you understand "blameless" to mean?

_____

_____

_____

Being "blameless" simply means that no one could point to this couple and accuse them of forsaking the moral laws of God. They did not willfully and intentionally sin. This obedient, godly couple "walked the talk."

How I pray that the people who know us best could say the same thing about us!

TRAVEL DIARY

Ponder this thought. If Dr. Luke were doing an investigation into your background, what would the eyewitnesses who interact with you say about you?

Would they say that you were righteous and blameless, keeping the Lord's commands? Could they say that they witness the love of God demonstrated in you? Would they say you are a woman of your word—a woman of integrity? Write your honest thoughts here:

_____

_____

_____

Take a moment to reflect on this…if we are going to prepare ourselves and other women for the return of Christ, we must be living witnesses of what He has done in our lives. We must be women of integrity.

In *The Purpose Driven Life*, Rick Warren says, "Before unbelievers accept the Bible as credible, they want to know that *we are*."

People in your circle of influence are desperately seeking the real deal—people who live what they believe. But how?

The apostle Paul says it best in Philippians 1:27a: "Whatever happens, conduct yourselves in a manner worthy of the gospel of Christ." God knows that how we handle heartaches, disappointments, successes, and our relationships with others is a testament of who we are.

Write that verse below in the form of a prayer, and let it become a lifestyle. Knowing how difficult this is to achieve, I'll pray for you and you pray for me!

_____

_____

_____

Once this verse becomes our lifestyle then we can be certain that should someone like Dr. Luke investigate our background and interview people who know us best, without hesitation they could say, "When it comes to her faith, she's the real deal—she walks the talk."

Dear one, many people in your circle of influence may never open a Bible. Therefore, diligently pray that you can be the living Word to them!

 ## TRAVELING MERCIES

Dear Father,
Help me to conduct myself in a manner worthy of the gospel. I earnestly
pray that others who know me will see by my actions and life that I
am a woman of integrity who demonstrates the love and the laws of
God. Amen.

SNAPSHOT

Live in such a way that those who know you, but don't know God, will come to know God because they know you.

WEEK 4, DAY 2
SECRET KEEPERS

SIGHTSEEING

If there was any doubt about friendship being God-ordained, one would only have to look at the lives of Elizabeth and Mary. Obviously, our God not only understood their need for a woman friend, He planned it! What brought these two women together were their unique circumstances—both were carrying a miracle child that would impact the future of the world. They were godly women with tremendous faith, yet they deeply needed someone to share in their experience—someone who understood. So, their loving heavenly Father gave them the perfect companion…He gave them each other.

I pray you appreciate how tender the heart of God is to meet this need in the lives of Elizabeth and Mary! God understands our need for intimacy. In fact, it's His idea.

Read Genesis 2:18. During the creation process, God said that everything was good, except one thing. What was that?

_____

Satan knows God's Word—unfortunately better than we do! Therefore, he will do everything he can to keep us alone and isolated. Often, when people face a difficult situation they withdraw, creating a perfect environment for Satan to work. Remember, his desire is to steal, kill, and destroy. His specialty is to wait until we are alone and then attack. We must be careful and not allow him to succeed.

One way to fight back is to make sure we have godly friends and relationships. God created us for relationship and fellowship, but healthy relationships require integrity. The dictionary defines integrity as "adherence to moral and ethical principles; soundness of moral character, honesty."

Pastor and author Charles Swindoll says the following, "Nothing speaks louder or more powerfully than a life of integrity." Godly men and women agree. Integrity is built slowly over a lifetime. It is a precious thing—difficult to build but easy to tear down. As believers in Christ, we must seek to live each day with discipline, honesty, and faith. When we do, at least two things happen: integrity becomes a habit, and we are blessed because of our obedience to God.

CONVERSATIONS

While Luke provides the conversation of Mary and Elizabeth's first moments, he never mentions the intimate details of Mary's visit. What took place during those three months remains unknown. What was said there stayed there, a good example for us to follow! The bond of trust between these two women had been established.

TRAVEL TIP

Before you share intimate details with others, make certain they have proven themselves trustworthy. These two women were able to express their greatest needs, hopes, and anxieties without any fear because they were women of integrity.

TRAVEL DIARY

Without hesitation, Mary shared her concerns with Elizabeth. What do you think they were?

_____

_____

_____

Likewise, Elizabeth felt safe to share with Mary her concerns. What do you think they were?

_____

_____

_____

Perhaps Mary shared concerns about her future, and Elizabeth shared heartache from her past. Isn't that what integrity allows—true intimacy? And isn't that what we desire in relationships—friends with whom we can share our deepest secrets, knowing that we can trust them completely?

Now for a hard question: Would Mary have been able to trust you with her secret?

Are you a person who keeps confidences?

What about the women you share life with? Are they women who are trustworthy?

Women long for intimate friendships, but without integrity it is impossible. A sister in Christ must be able to go to a prayer partner and pour out her heart without fear that what she shares will be repeated. *Girlfriends keep secrets.*

I learned of a survey of over 40,000 women where the number one reason given for the demise of a best friend was betrayal. Have you ever experienced the pain of betrayal by a close friend?

Were you able to move past it and move forward?

It is essential that we forgive, let go of the hurt, and move on. That is very difficult to do, but God is willing and able to help.

Jesus understood the pain of betrayal because a close friend betrayed Him. Do you remember who it was? (To refresh your memory look at Matthew 26:17-30 and 47-50.) _____

When we share our secrets, hurts, and confidences with a best friend, we never expect that friend to repeat them with someone else. Read the following and decide if you agree with it:

> I have no respect for justice and no mercy for defenseless humanity. I ruin without killing. I tear down homes. I break hearts and wreck lives. You will find me in the pews of the pious as well as in the haunts of the unholy. I gather strength with age. I have made my way where greed, distrust, and dishonor are unknown; yet my victims are as numerous as the sands of the sea, and often as innocent. My name is gossip.

Do I hear a hearty "Amen?" Gossip is devastating and an easy trap to fall into. We must be alert and not fall prey to the scheme of the enemy. Neither should we be misled into thinking that gossip means only untruths spread about others. Gossip is defined as "idle talk or rumor, especially about the personal or private affairs of others."

When a friend betrays us and trust is gone, it's extremely difficult to build back. In many cases the relationship is never the same. If we are going to have a real impact for God's kingdom, we must be extremely careful and not allow ourselves to be swept away by gossip. God has a much higher standard for His followers. We are to be women of integrity.

When Mary stood in the doorway of Elizabeth's home, her secret was safe. Because of Elizabeth's integrity she had the honor of mentoring the mother of God's Son.

Girlfriend…be like Elizabeth. Keep secrets. Who knows when a young woman like Mary will show up at your door—a woman with the biggest secret since the beginning of time.

TRAVELING MERCIES

Dear Father,
Keep a guard over my mouth and help me to be a secret keeper. Never let me be one that talks about others. When I am tempted, quicken my spirit for I know this is not pleasing to You. May I instead speak uplifting, truthful, and fitting words and demonstrate trustworthiness and integrity in my relationships. Amen.

SNAPSHOT

Confess your sins…not your neighbors!

TRAVEL ADVISORY

It is important to mention that there are some situations that we cannot keep to ourselves, situations that might include domestic violence, suicidal tendencies, drug abuse, or any situation where you believe your friend is in danger. Usually this situation can be handled with wisdom and without betraying her confidence. Here are some guidelines:

1. Be honest with her. Suggest professional help.

2. Provide the names of agencies, pastors, or other professionals who specialize in her need of expertise.

3. Pray together.

4. Make certain she understands that your concern is from pure motives and (unless you are a professional counselor) you do not have the expertise or solution to her problems. So point her in the right direction, helping her understand that you are acting in true friendship by helping her deal with the issue.

WEEK 4, DAY 3
WHEN WE SAY I DO: INTEGRITY IN MARRIAGE

SIGHTSEEING

Scripture Reading: Luke 1:11-25

While our study focuses on the relationship between Mary and Elizabeth, there is also another important person in the family dynamic—Zechariah. I have a deep respect for him. In fact, if you are single, pray that if God should lead you into marriage someday, that He will lead you to a man like Zechariah!

Writing this study required many hours of research, and I learned some hard truths about the culture in which Mary and Elizabeth lived. It also helped me to better understand the kind of man Elizabeth was married to. Since marriage is such a critical part of our own society, I felt it deserved some attention.

Did you know that Elizabeth's inability to produce a child provided Zechariah grounds for divorce? As we learned earlier, this culture had a strong mindset regarding the importance of having an heir. The Old Testament provides several examples of men in the Jewish culture who had multiple wives or maidservants. You may be familiar with the stories of Sarah and Hagar; Jacob's two wives, Leah and Rebecca; and Hannah, the mother of Samuel.

My personal interpretation of the Scriptures makes me think that Zechariah was a tender man, but also tough. After all, he argued with an angel (Luke 1:18). While Scripture doesn't give specifics about Gabriel's appearance, his name means "God is my strength!" Still, Zechariah stood his stubborn, but foolish, ground when the angel told him, "You are going to have a son."

I admire many things about this godly priest. The fact that he honored his marriage covenant with Elizabeth, though he had legal grounds to divorce her, ranks at the top of my list.

CONVERSATIONS

While there is debate about the actual percentage of divorces in America, and among Christians, it is understood that divorce is far too common. This is not what our heavenly Father had in mind when creating marriage. (See Genesis 2:24, Matthew 5:31-32, Matthew 19:3-6.) I recently learned about a new trend that stunned me: "starter marriages." I had heard of starter houses, but never starter marriages. It seems that today's generation has bought into a philosophy that divorce is inevitable! Yet, as believers, we cannot! We must remain faithful to God's standard for marriage and our vows of "until death do us part."

Let me be clear. I understand that sometimes there is no alternative but divorce. I am a product of divorce. I am grateful that my mother had the courage to divorce my father in a time when that was unacceptable in Christian circles. However, I also know the pain, hardship, and lasting imprints divorce leaves on children. This girl understands the Scripture in Malachi 2:16a: "I hate divorce," says the LORD God of Israel ..." If you have been through a divorce and survived it, then you know why.

God is looking for godly couples like Elizabeth and Zechariah, who honor their covenant with Him and each other...not to endure a life of dysfunction, suffering, and betrayal, but to experience a blessed life where the two become one, walking side-by-side...a marriage whose foundation is built on the principles of God.

Yes, marriage is work, but the benefits are beyond our comprehension. This statement comes from a woman who was a bride at 18 and has been married for over 35 years. Like *all* married couples, my husband and I have had our struggles. Are you familiar with the Scripture about not letting the "sun go down on your wrath?" (Ephesians 4:26). I jokingly say we didn't. We never went to bed mad. We just stayed up and fought all night!

Life brings many challenges that will test even the strongest marriages. When our most difficult time came and we were almost ready to give up, we decided to seek the help of a Christian counselor. His expertise and guidance helped us to realize God's instructions for marriage. Due to the demands of life we had just gotten off course and lost our way. Faithfully we prayed and put God at the center of our marriage. It was hard work, but anything worth achieving is. Now, 25 years later, we are living proof that marriage is one of God's greatest gifts.

If you are at a place in your marriage where you feel out of love, or unloved, or just ready to call it quits, seek God diligently in the matter. Reconciliation is His specialty. Allow Him to lead you in the direction that you should go. Don't be afraid to seek counseling—just make sure it is faith-based and that the counselor is a professional and highly recommended. Don't give up your marriage without a fight!

TRAVEL DIARY

Traditional marriage is under attack in our country. Therefore, as believers, we must demonstrate God's definition of what He had in mind when He said, that "two shall become one."

What is God's definition of marriage?

Please look up Genesis 2:21-24.

_____

_____

_____

How did God create woman?

_____

_____

_____

What did God state about a man's relationship with the woman?

_____

_____

_____

What were the two to become?_____

While many in America debate the definition of marriage, we see here its beautiful beginning. God created Eve out of the framework of Adam, his side. He emphasized the oneness a man and woman should have, not simply a contract or partnership. He laid the groundwork for a man to emotionally leave other ties and become one with his wife. This is a beautiful picture of mutual love and respect, a oneness of body, mind, and spirit.

As the eyes of our nation watch those of us who believe in traditional marriage (that marriage is holy and sacred and between one man and one woman), may we faithfully and boldly become the Zechariahs and Elizabeths of the 21st century. May we be people of integrity who honor their covenant with God and with each other.

If you are married, take a few moments to reflect on your marriage. Does it demonstrate the oneness God intends? _____

How?

_____

_____

_____

What areas could be improved?

_____ better communication

_____ more expressions of affection

_____ more complimentary speech

_____ more time together

_____ more fun

Choose one and make a genuine effort toward improvement, starting with you! Perhaps this would be a good time to focus on your marriage, and rediscover all the blessings that God intended. There are marriage retreats and conferences that can really add a spark to your relationship.

If you are single, and hoping someday to enter marriage, seek God's wisdom and guidance for your life. Until then, please do all that you can to help preserve the *sanctity* of marriage. What are some unique ways that you can encourage your married friends?

Write some thoughts about this.

_____

_____

_____

Traveling Mercies

Dear Father,

Thank You for the beautiful partnership of marriage and for the example of Zachariah and Elizabeth. May we as the Body of Christ maintain the same level of commitment to the sanctity of marriage. Amen.

Snapshot

A good marriage is like a good trade. Each thinks he got the better deal. (Ivern Ball, American Author)

WEEK 4, DAY 4
INTEGRITY OF THE SABBATH: SABBATH SISTERS

🚌 SIGHTSEEING

We've covered a lot of territory during our friendship journey. In fact, we've gone at record speed. That's the reason I've decided to revisit a place in Scripture that we may have overlooked. It has a tremendous significance.

We are back in Jerusalem at the temple. Gabriel has just arrived. A faithful priest has no idea that today God will break His silence and reveal His plan for eternal salvation! The stage is set and the main players are in place.

Please return to Luke 1:8-10 and meditate a few moments on these verses.

Notice in verse 8 *where* God sent the angel Gabriel to meet Zechariah.

Zechariah was chosen to go into the _____.

Don't miss the significance of that. After 400 years of silence, God is ready to speak. Amazingly, he chose the temple which historically was the center of corporate worship.

God had spoken from mountains, burning bushes, and even through a stubborn donkey. Yet when He was ready to break His silence and present His plan of the coming Messiah, He chose the temple (the church). That alone should demonstrate the important role the Church would play in Christianity.

Now, notice God's timing—*when* He spoke. We see this in verse 10: "And when the time for the burning of incense came, all the assembled worshipers were praying outside."

Have you noticed that throughout Scripture, *timing* is more important to God than *time?*

This was their Sabbath day, and even though God's people had abandoned and forsaken His laws, this one remained dear in their culture. "Remember the Sabbath day and keep it holy" (Exodus 20:8). It was a day set apart, an example demonstrated by God from the beginning of time. In Hebrew, the original language of the Old Testament, the word Sabbath means to "cease or rest"—literally, to stop.

Let's read Isaiah 58:13-14 from The Message:

> If you watch your step on the Sabbath, and don't use my holy day for personal advantage,

> If you treat the Sabbath as a day of joy, God's holy day as a celebration,
> If you honor it by refusing "business as usual," making money, running
> here and there—
> Then you'll be free to enjoy God! Oh, I'll make you ride high and soar
> above it all.
> I'll make you feast on the inheritance of your ancestor, Jacob. Yes! God
> says so!

God tells us that we will find joy in the Lord by honoring the Sabbath day.

That settles it, girls. I'm starting a new trend: Invite Your Girlfriends to Church Day! It's a sure prescription for joy.

CONVERSATIONS

Psalm 139:14 states that we are "fearfully and wonderfully made." God is our Creator and therefore knows we need rest.

When God delivered His people out of bondage and established the ten most important guidelines for life, number four on the list was to set aside one day a week for rest. While the Israelites were in Egypt under Pharaoh's command, they never had a day off. Every day they worked from sun up until sun down.

Look at the following two scriptures:

> Remember that you were slaves in Egypt and that the LORD your God brought you out of there with a mighty hand and an outstretched arm. Therefore the LORD your God has commanded you to observe the Sabbath day. (Deuteronomy 5:15)

> He said to them, "This is what the LORD commanded: 'Tomorrow is to be a day of rest, a holy Sabbath to the LORD. So bake what you want to bake and boil what you want to boil. Save whatever is left and keep it until morning.'" (Exodus 16:23)

I love this scripture. It clearly points out that women were invited to have a Sabbath day of rest as well. God saw the value in what women did long before society did.

When Christ came to earth, He knew that the religious zealots had added so many ridiculous attachments that honoring the Sabbath had become a burden. They had taken something God meant for our good and completely abused it. Read what Christ said about that from Mark 2:27: "Then he said to them, 'The

Sabbath was made for man, not man for the Sabbath.'" Again we see that our Creator had our best interests in mind. In today's society, however, we have gone to the other extreme. We have misused and abused God's grace and take little or no time to honor the Sabbath.

I am fully aware that we are not under the old law. The indwelling of God's Spirit has brought a new way for Christians to fulfill the desires of God through His love. However, the new covenant does not invalidate the relevance of the Ten Commandments. They pertained to God's desires for His people. As much as it remains God's desire for man not to kill, steal or commit adultery, God also desires for believers to show their love for Him and honor Him on a day reserved for Him.

Going to church is also a matter of obeying God's Word. Read Hebrews 10:24-25:

> And let us consider how we may spur one another on toward love and good deeds. Let us not give up meeting together, as some are in the habit of doing, but let us encourage one another—and all the more as you see the day approaching.

Girlfriends, we need each other. Some of the best friendships you will ever enjoy are those you make in the body of Christ. I call them "Sistahs in the Faith!"

A pastor I greatly respect pointed out that everywhere the apostles went, the first thing they did was to win converts and establish a church. They knew that believers could not survive without a church body. In Matthew 16:18, Jesus said to Peter, "...and on this rock, I shall build my church and the gates of Hades will not overcome it." How wonderful it is to know that nothing will ever destroy God's Church.

If you have given up on church because of a negative experience, or if you wonder if going to church is necessary, just remember that going to church sure paid off for Zechariah! So get on back to church, girlfriend ...you never know who might show up!

Travel Diary

Do you think the Body of Christ honors the integrity of the Sabbath day in the 21st century?

If yes, how? If no, why not?

_____

_____

_____

Are you glad God set aside a day for worship and rest? _____

Why? _____

_____

_____

Is it hard for you to set aside this day for God? _____

Why? _____

_____

_____

What do you think would happen if the Body of Christ allowed Sunday to be a day of worship, rest, and fellowship—a day to cease normal activities, and honor God?

_____

_____

_____

How could honoring the Sabbath day have a positive impact on:

You? _____

Your family? _____

Your community? _____

Our culture? _____

Would there be any negative impact? _____

 ## TRAVELING MERCIES

> Lord,
> In our world that never stops, please show me how to honor the Sabbath
> day. Thank You for providing a day of rest for me in Your divine plan.
> Help me as Your child to keep this day holy. Amen.

SNAPSHOT

If the God of all creation took a day to rest, how can we do any less?

WEEK 4, DAY 5
BONUS MILES: THE FRIENDS WE CHOOSE

SIGHTSEEING

In the first chapter of week one, we discussed the definition of a friend. Today we are going to look at the different levels of friendship. I pray that you will find this very intriguing and life changing.

There are three basic levels of friendships:

1. Acquaintances
2. Good friends
3. Soul mates

Acquaintances represent the large group of people we meet during life, people we know, but not intimately. These may include our neighbors, the waitress/waiter in our favorite eating establishment, or the teller at the bank.

We interact on a surface level with these people. We don't choose them—they just happen to be in our lives due to daily activities.

Good friends are drawn from our circle of acquaintances. These are the people you would invite to your baby shower, 25th wedding anniversary party, or to whom you would send Christmas cards. Unlike acquaintances, we *choose* to have these people as part of our lives. We may share similar beliefs, values, common interests, or hobbies. We enjoy their company. Good friends are different from acquaintances because we have gone beyond the surface with them.

These relationships develop from circumstances that have provided opportunities for you to be together and develop a heart connection. This often happens with mothers who have children the same age, coworkers who share projects, Sunday school classmates who are about the same age or at the same stage of life, or people who share hobbies and activities.

And then there are soul mates—best friends.

A soul mate doesn't happen overnight. In fact, it takes time to build this kind of relationship. I believe soul mates are a gift from God. They are precious and few. They give you strength, encouragement, and contribute to your life. Mary and Elizabeth were soul mates.

Jesus had many acquaintances and good friends, but He had only three soul mates. Can you remember who they were?

Peter, James, and John shared some of Christ's most significant moments. I love the fact that Jesus had three—not just one—soul mates. Often females from the time we are little girls think we need only one "best friend," but that isn't necessarily best. I have four soul mates (one of them is my husband!). All of my soul mates are very different but contribute to my life in vital ways. They keep me balanced and make my life richer.

As soul mates we have shared more than activities—we have shared intimacy. We have gone far below the surface together. For those of us who desire meaningful relationships like this, God has provided specific guidelines. If applied they can take our relationships to a whole other level.

CONVERSATIONS

1. First we must have a right relationship with God.

It is interesting to note that when Elizabeth discovered that she was with child, she remained in seclusion for five months (Luke 1:24). I believe she was pursuing a deeper relationship with God in preparation for her calling. After she did this, her soul mate, Mary, the mother of her Lord, arrived.

I have been blessed to have a godly mother who has been my best friend since the day I was born. She knows all of my secrets and loves me unconditionally. Over the years, her love filled my need for a "best friend" and still does.

But, life changes. When I was 35, my mother remarried and moved out of state. What an adjustment! She had been a single mom for most of my life. Her children had been her primary focus. She had lived only five miles up the road and I talked with her daily. Now, she had a husband, and lived 60 miles away.

During those lonely months of adjustments, we learned that God wanted us to depend on Him—He wanted first place. I found I had grown so dependent on Mom that I would call her with my concerns before going to God or His Word.

After this growing period in which we learned to give God first place, He broadened our circle of good friends, and added soul mates. These women have blessed our lives immensely. Now we both keep God first and enjoy terrific friendships.

2. Once we have developed a right relationship with God, we must seek His counsel and ask Him to bring the right people into our lives.

Before Jesus selected His disciples, He prayed. Since the Son of God sought the wise counsel of His Father regarding friendship, we should too.

3. Practice discernment.

Proverbs 12:26 tells us, "A righteous man is cautious in friendship but the way of the wicked leads them astray." Girlfriend, we need to be cautious of who we invite to be our good friends and soul mates. Friends have a powerful influence on us.

Sometimes in our loneliness we become so needy for companionship that we let our guard down and begin to associate with people that the Lord would not approve of. Can you recall a time when you associated with someone that you knew did not have the same values as you? Briefly describe the situation.

_____

_____

_____

Were there any negative consequences?

_____

_____

_____

In 1 Corinthians 5:11 the apostle Paul provided specific guidelines for followers of Christ: "I am writing you that you must not associate with anyone who calls himself a brother but is sexually immoral or greedy, an idolater or a slanderer, a drunkard or a swindler. With such a man do not even eat."

How does this Scripture speak to you about the people we associate with?

_____

_____

_____

The key word is "associate," which means "to participate in activity." Certainly we are to *love* all people, as Christ did. However, like Christ, we must use discernment when deciding whom we will allow into our most intimate circle of friends. Paul is very clear about his feelings on loving others. He is the author of 1 Corinthians 13. But the point Paul is making here is that we are not to choose a soul mate, or good friend, who is involved in an ungodly lifestyle. This doesn't mean we are to be rude or unfriendly. It means we must use discernment in our choices. Not all people make good friends.

My background is in arts and entertainment. I worked with some of the most talented—and brilliant—artists in the dance industry. I thoroughly enjoyed working with them and admired their talent greatly, but our values were quiet different. They knew it, and so did I. They were my professional coworkers but God rarely allowed me to socialize with them. During our time together, I did my best to demonstrate integrity, love, and friendship, and I believe it had a positive effect on them. However, I was very careful to guard my heart.

From the time our children are little, we caution them about choosing friends because we know that wrong influences can lead them down the wrong path. We are God's children, and in His love, for us He specifically warns us to be careful about our relationships.

If you have some close friends in your life who are bad influences and prevent you from becoming the woman that God desires, take this matter before Him regularly. I understand it would be difficult to suddenly "drop them." But, if you begin to make godly choices and stand firm on God's Word in front of them, the relationship will change. Either they will want what you have, or they will feel so uncomfortable around you that they will "drop you" and seek friends who enjoy the same kind of lifestyle they do.

Always remember that God wants us to share life with others and enjoy the blessings of truly good friends. God wants the best for you!

4. Finally, give your good friends and soul mates the grace to be human.

As we apply these guidelines, remember that we are all sinners saved by grace. We each make plenty of mistakes. So, as you choose your friends wisely, also choose to forgive generously.

Travel Diary

Girlfriend's Checklist

Do I have godly friends that encourage me to make smart choices? _____

Do the women I associate with have godly values? _____

Do my good friends pray for me and encourage me to be all that I can be in Christ? _____

Could I go to my friends and ask for prayer and know that they would pray? _____

Do my friends celebrate with me in success, weep with me in grief? Do they provide loving and godly instruction when I need it? _____

Our life journey is short. We will be here for a brief time. Therefore, seek God diligently to provide the people who can help you to become more like Jesus.

Traveling Mercies

Dear Father,
Thank You for the amazing gift of friendship and the wonderful people You have allowed me to share life with. As I consider my circle of friends, and seek to expand it, please give me wisdom. Help me be a woman of integrity, a good friend to others, and help me choose godly women who desire that as well. Thank You for being the Best Friend of all. Amen.

Snapshot

A soul mate is the kind of friend who sends a postcard while on vacation that says, "Wish you were here!"—and means it.

Women Who Encourage

I pray that our trip has been a wonderful learning experience and that you are ready for our next stop: Encouragement Avenue!

Wouldn't it be wonderful if there really were an Encouragement Avenue, a place where a weary soul could stop, be encouraged, and run the race that God has planned for us?

Mary found her place at the home of Elizabeth where she received an ample supply of love and grace for God's high calling.

God has placed a high calling on our lives to be encouragers, so meet me in the neighborhood to learn all that we can. The address is 101 Encouragement Avenue!

ITINERARY

Day 1–The Encourager

Day 2–The Power of a Positive Friend

Day 3–Lean on Me

Day 4 –Word Power: I Can't Believe I Said That!

 TRAVEL TIP

> *"Let us consider how we may spur one another on toward love and good deeds. Let us not give up meeting together as some are in the habit of doing, but let us encourage one another, and all the more as you see the day approaching" (Hebrews 10:24-25).*

WEEK 5, DAY 1
THE ENCOURAGER

A REST STOP

I travel quite a bit. Nothing is more thrilling or more tiring. Since we've been on this journey for a few weeks now, I thought today we'd depart from our usual route of sightseeing and conversations and pull over for a much needed rest and enjoy the view. After reading today's lesson you might like to revisit our scripture at Luke 1:30-45.

When I began writing today's lesson, I paused and asked God to give me a more intimate understanding of our Scripture passage. I sensed He wanted us to relate to Elizabeth and Mary as women. So, with the heavenly Father's permission and under the power of the Holy Spirit, I have blended my imagination with Scripture. Being so familiar with the text, you will know where Scripture ends and my imagination begins.

It is my prayer that you can visualize the following:

It is almost evening, the end of another day as Elizabeth reflects over all that has happened in the last six months. Now heavy with child and barely able to see her toes, she smiles and thinks, *I am probably the only expectant mother who feels her time is passing too quickly.*

Pregnancy certainly agreed with her. Her body adjusted to the changes, and she welcomed each of them. From the time she was a young girl she had dreamed of being a mother. This was her moment—her calling. She would not trade it for anything! During these months of seclusion, God had revealed Himself in ways that amazed her. It was both holy and miraculous.

Her household was so quiet. The only way Zechariah could communicate was to scribble a note to her. And, who could read his writing! It was barely legible. Still, when he penned the intimate details of the angel's visit, she could not get enough. She carefully engraved every word upon her heart so that someday, she could share this with her son.

She missed the sound of her beloved's voice. No one said her name the way that he did. No one laughed so richly and so deeply. She knew his silence served as a reminder that Jehovah God was the one true God. To think that she and Zechariah would be the parents of a prophet still amazed them! What's a little loneliness and seclusion compared to that? Her religious background had taught her that sometimes God requires sacrifice. But today, her heart ached for feminine companionship and conversation. How nice it would be to share her experience with another woman, but whom?

Who could possibly understand the wonder of her miraculous pregnancy? Who could relate with the joy she experienced, knowing that before the foundations of the earth were created, God had chosen her to be the mother of the forerunner for the Messiah?

In her village, she had been known as Elizabeth, "the barren one," and had never been part of the secrets expectant mothers shared. She had no experience in childbirth, but she knew God would work things out. She had fully accepted that even if no other woman would share this journey with her, the heavenly Father had blessed her beyond measure; and isolation was a small price to pay for the honor bestowed upon her.

Elizabeth had grown so accustomed to the silence in her home that the knock at the door startled her. While she slowly stood to get her balance, Zechariah opened the door. Standing at the threshold was a young girl, very timid and so small. She looked familiar, but Elizabeth could not recall who she was.

At first, the young girl said nothing, but stared at Elizabeth's swollen belly so obvious with child. Suddenly, tears spilled from her eyes as she spoke:

"Greetings, Zechariah. Greetings, Elizabeth. It is Mary, your relative, daughter of Henli!"

When Elizabeth heard Mary's greeting, something happened. The baby in her womb leaped, and she was filled with the Holy Spirit. It was unlike anything she had experienced during her pregnancy.

Stretching open arms toward the young woman, she proclaimed, "Blessed are you among women and blessed is the child you will bear! However, why am I so favored that the mother of my Lord should come to me!?"

Embracing Mary with all the tenderness of a wise and experienced woman, she continued to pour out a blessing on the mother of God's Son.

"Blessed is she who has believed that what the Lord has said unto her will be accomplished!"

With those words, all fear vanished from the young virgin. What the angel had said was true! Elizabeth was pregnant. Gazing upon her face, Mary thought, *She is the most beautiful mother-to-be I've ever seen—radiant, glowing, and overflowing with joy!*

The two women held each other more tightly, realizing they had experienced the manifestations of God's love. All along He knew their need for feminine companionship and intimacy, and He had provided.

So overcome with emotion that neither could speak, they simply bowed before their God, giving Him praise and gratitude, realizing in the midst of their calling He had given them the perfect companion. He gave them each other.

TRAVEL DIARY

I doubt that Mary ever forgot the warm embrace of Elizabeth's arms and her powerful encouragement. Often, we do forget. Over time we forget the special people who helped us through an extremely difficult time. Perhaps someone stopped by for a visit, called us on the phone, or sent a card or an e-mail with the perfect words.

Today I would like to encourage you to take a moment and remember some people who you should never forget, people who provided encouragement when you needed it the most. Perhaps it was a family member, a schoolteacher, a best friend, a neighbor, or a church member.

Please write their names and what they did to encourage you.

1. _____

   _____

2. _____

   _____

3. _____

   _____

4. _____

   _____

Say a prayer of thanksgiving to God for placing them in your life at a time when you needed someone to help bear your burdens. Now it's your turn—go and do likewise.

TRAVELING MERCIES

Dear Father,
 Thank You for the many people You have placed in my life that have encouraged me when I needed it the most. I ask You to bless them as they have blessed me. Father, help me to be a woman who encourages others. Amen.

SNAPSHOT

"...he who refreshes others will himself be refreshed" (Proverbs 11:25b NIV).

WEEK 5, DAY 2
THE POWER OF A POSITIVE FRIEND

🖼 SIGHTSEEING

Don't you just love to be around positive people—those special people who always see the good in spite of the circumstances? It does something to our souls. It gives us hope.

Question: When do people need encouragement the most?
Answer: When the circumstances are the worst.

That isn't easy. It's difficult to offer words of encouragement when the bottom has just dropped out. It's much easier to dwell on the negative and point out the worst. But how does that help a hurting soul?

Usually, people know how bad things are. What they need is a reminder of how good God is, and that nothing is too difficult for Him. They need encouragement.

As we learned yesterday, the perfect example of a woman who understood and demonstrated encouragement is Elizabeth. Let's read her encouraging words to Mary in Luke 1:41-45.

When Mary arrived at Elizabeth's, circumstances were amazing but alarming. Let's look at the facts. Mary was pregnant, unmarried, and very young. She knew nothing about being a wife or mother and lived in a culture that stoned women who became pregnant out of wedlock! Honestly, that's about as bad as it gets! Yet, when we read Elizabeth's greeting, we find not a hint of negativity. Why not?

I believe Elizabeth remained centered on the fact that God was in control no matter how things appeared. God would take care of every concern. He was well aware of the facts! So, instead of speaking words of doom and gloom, she spoke words of praise and affirmation. But how?

Luke 1:41 gives us the answer. She was filled with the _____ _____

Elizabeth allowed the Holy Spirit to speak through her. Girlfriend—let's apply that wise lesson from our mentor—let the Holy Spirit do the talking!

In reality, the days ahead for Mary would be extremely difficult. She would face many obstacles and challenges, but Elizabeth understood that God was far greater than any circumstance.

People in our circle need to know this as well. God is greater than divorce, sickness, poverty, children who are in trouble, and all the other heartaches in life.

Charles Swindoll says, "To encourage another is to breathe courage into them." What a beautiful thought. I think that's what Elizabeth did for Mary.

CONVERSATIONS

One of the most memorable scenes from the movie *Steel Magnolias* takes place at a cemetery. M'Lynn, played by Sally Field, has just buried her adult daughter after years of illness. It is perhaps the darkest moment any mother could experience.

All family members have left the graveside except M' Lynn and her four best friends. They don't know what to say. No one ever does in times like these. Their attempts are sincere and even humorous. However, they are there, fully aware that they cannot change the circumstances. So they did what they could do. They stood with her in her darkest hour, which breathed courage into her. These dear friends didn't ignore the facts. They knew that dark days were ahead for M'Lynn and they would be there, walking beside her.

If encouragement does not come naturally for you, I understand. Perhaps you were never encouraged or maybe you are immersed in a negative environment. So, would you allow me to offer some words of encouragement?

With God's help and a willing heart, you *can* overcome a negative spirit. God placed this study in your life at this particular time. I am certain that He is ready to help you become a woman who encourages others. As you encourage others, you will be encouraged! (Proverbs 11:25)

Start today! Be alert and look for the good in others. Remind yourself that God is greater than any circumstance.

TRAVEL DIARY

Definition: "to encourage"

1. *Give somebody hope, confidence or courage.*

2. *Urge or motivate someone to do something.*

Today's questions are designed to help you make encouragement a *lifestyle.*

When the bottom seems to fall out, what is the first thing I do?

_____

_____

_____

Am I able to remind my friends of God's goodness in a compassionate way?

_____

_____

_____

Am I a person who encourages my friends even when circumstances look difficult?

_____

_____

_____

Do I have trouble seeing good in the most difficult situations?

_____ Why? _____

_____

_____

Do I allow the negative opinions of others to influence me?

_____ Who specifically_____

_____

Negativity and feelings of defeat are everywhere. Be careful! These are contagious and old tricks used by Satan. We must be on guard!

Satan knows that he cannot steal our salvation, but he will stop at nothing to steal our joy. If he can steal our joy, he can steal our strength. Nehemiah 8:10 says, "For the joy of the LORD is your strength."

When negative thoughts come into your mind, stop. Take a breath. Ask God to remind you that Jesus came "so that you might have life and enjoy it to the full" (John 10:10 NIV). "Greater is He that is in you than he that is in the world" (1 John 4:4 NIV).

Need some practice on encouraging others? Take a minute and think about the people in your circle of influence: family, friends, pastor, church staff, coworkers, neighbors. Think about all the responsibilities they have. We don't have to wonder if they could use encouragement—we know they could. Choose one from your list and give them a call, or send them a short note of encouragement.

Knowing personally how encouragement strengthens us, pray earnestly for God to help you become an encourager—one who brings some needed CPR (Christ-like Positive Refreshment).

TRAVELING MERCIES

Dear Father,
You are a God who encourages! We know that life is hard, but You are good. Your Word says that we can do all things through Christ who strengthens us (Philippians 4:13). Father, help me to be a person of encouragement. Whenever my friends are struggling and life hurts, help me to remind them of all that You have done! Amen.

SNAPSHOT

"Man's highest duty is to encourage others." (Charles Swindoll)

WEEK 5, DAY 3
LEAN ON ME

SIGHTSEEING

Today in our friendship journey we will travel down the pathway of prayer. There's nothing we can do for our friends that is more powerful or more important than prayer.

Our Scripture reading is Mark 14:32-41. Invite the Holy Spirit to breathe fresh insights as you read this familiar passage.

In verse 34, Jesus tells His three best friends (His soul mates), "My soul is overwhelmed with sorrow to the point of death. Stay here and keep watch"(NIV). Jesus shared His heartache and simply asked them to pray. Our Savior knew the power of prayer and that prayer doesn't change God, it changes us.

On the night our Lord requested prayer, unfortunately, his best friends didn't meet that need. This scene will forever break our hearts, each time we read it.

Make no mistake—Jesus understood His purpose. He came for one reason only, to take away the sins of the world. That required His death. He knew His time had come. What He wanted from His disciples was prayer. In Luke 22:40 we read what Jesus specifically asked them to pray. "Pray that you will not fall into temptation" (NIV).

Jesus knew that overwhelming circumstances lay ahead for His disciples. He knew that prayer was the only thing that would sustain them.

Continue reading through verse 44.

Luke's version paints the agony of Christ's prayer, with wails of grief and sweat like "drops of blood." It also shows the mercy of God. When others abandon us, God doesn't.

What did God do for His beloved Son in verse 43?

_____

This tender picture of God's angels ministering to God's Son, shows us God's unfailing love. Should you be abandoned by family and friends, be assured that your loving Father will never leave you nor forsake you (Deuteronomy 31:6, 8; Joshua 1:5; Hebrews 13:5).

Stop for a moment and allow your imagination to picture the angels ministering to God's Son. Record your thoughts:

_____

_____

_____

Did they hold Him? Did they sing Him a Psalm? Did they encourage Him? Certainly, these are thoughts to ponder.

CONVERSATIONS

As I am writing this Bible study, my niece's six-year-old daughter has Batten's disease. It is terminal and will take her from us much too soon. As women, none of us can imagine anything worse than losing a child. Nothing causes us to question our faith more than watching a child suffer.

The circumstances are overwhelmingly bleak. Nothing I say or do will change them. I can offer no explanations. However, I must focus on who God is and what I *can* do. I *can* encourage her to allow God to be God. I *can* provide a shoulder to cry on and arms to hold her. She *can* lean on me, and I will lean on God.

Someday the circumstances may be reversed, and I will lean on her. That's the way it is in the Body of Christ...the way God intended.

At times, we feel completely helpless and don't know what to do. However, God has invited us to come boldly before His throne and lean on His everlasting arms. It is the best thing we can do for others.

James 5:16 in the Amplified Bible says, "The earnest (heartfelt, continued) prayer of a righteous man makes tremendous power available (dynamic in its working)."

How important is prayer to God?

Since the beginning of our study, we have camped in the first chapter of the Gospel of Luke. Let's return there just a moment and notice two places where prayer is mentioned. The first one is in Luke 1:9. What are the people doing outside the temple?

_____

Just think, on the day that God breaks His silence after 400 years, His people "just happen" to be praying. Some scholars say that the people were face down, crying out to God.

Now, let's look at Luke 1:13. When the angel Gabriel appeared in the temple, he says, "Fear not Zechariah, your _____ have been heard" (NIV). The angel assured Zechariah that God had heard his prayers.

This was the first thing the angel Gabriel wanted the faithful priest to know. Powerful thought, isn't it? In fact, it makes my heart smile! Guess what, dear one, your prayers have been heard, too! You must believe that.

Have you experienced answers to prayer?

_____

Are you a person your girlfriends can call for prayer and know that you will pray?

_____

I have personally experienced the power of prayer. I was deathly sick and unable to pray for myself. However, my sisters in Christ interceded for me. Clothed in the armor of God with swords drawn and shields held high, they faithfully brought my name before the throne of God, praying fervently without ceasing. I cannot find the words to express my gratitude. I received a miraculous healing. Girlfriends, let us never underestimate the power of prayer.

Travel Diary

Can you recall a time when you desperately needed prayer? Please describe.

_____

_____

_____

Do you have a prayer partner, someone that you can call upon day or night to intercede on your behalf? I pray that you do. If not, ask God to send you a prayer partner and trust Him to answer this prayer.

We can only imagine the sweet moments of prayer that Mary and Elizabeth shared. The intimacy of prayer is powerful. How it must have encouraged them.

Is someone in your life going through a difficult situation? Pray for her without ceasing. Allow her to lean on you as you lean on God. Cling to the words of Gabriel, "Your prayers have been heard."

TRAVELING MERCIES

> *Dear Father,*
> *Thank you for prayer and that you are a God who desires communication with His people. Your Word tells us that as believers we can come to You with confidence.*

This is the confidence we have in approaching God; that if we ask anything according to His will He hears us. And if we know that He hears us—whatever we ask—we know that we have what we asked of Him (1 John 5:14-15 NIV).

SNAPSHOT

Prayer doesn't change God…it changes us.

WEEK 5, DAY 4
WORD POWER—I CAN'T BELIEVE I SAID THAT!

SIGHTSEEING

For our Scripture reading, we will travel to the book of James, written by the brother of Jesus. While writing this particular passage, I believe James was speaking from experience, as one who understood the power of the tongue. He had witnessed what it had done to his beloved brother and Savior. He wanted followers of Christ to know that the tongue is a powerful instrument that can be used for good or for evil. We choose.

Now, let's turn in our Bibles and read James 3:1-12.

There's an old saying: "Words are cheap, but once spoken, they can cost dearly." Think for a moment about the power of words and what they can do.

Proverbs 18:21 (NIV) says, "The tongue has the power of life and death." What does that mean to you?

At a moment's notice we can recall harsh words others have said to us. Words so painful, they almost stripped us of any self-esteem we possessed. How many times did we replay their words in our minds? How many times did we believe them?

If words can lift us up, they can also tear us down. When I was a teenager in the late 60s, I was practically legally blind and wore thick glasses with black pointed frames. I was teased so severely that whenever I walked down the hall or went to any social event, I didn't wear my glasses in fear of being called "four eyes." The kids didn't know how badly their words wounded my heart. They weren't even thinking.

Unfortunately, I also have said things that hurt and offended others many times. What's so amazing is that most often, I didn't really mean what I said. The words just slipped out. Sometimes I wanted to grab my mouth and cry… "I can't believe I said that!" Other times, I allowed either anger, fatigue, a bad mood, or my own hurt feelings to speak for me. I realized too late that my words were so hurtful I might as well have thrown stones. How I wish I could take every one of them back. You too?

Regrettably, we can't. However, we can thank God that His mercies are new every day. He is a God of second chances, willing and able to help us speak words that affirm and encourage. We must be willing to make this a priority.

 ## CONVERSATIONS

Taming the Tongue—The Words We Use

What does verse 6 say about the tongue?

_____

_____

_____

What can fire do? _____

_____

_____

Fire provides warmth when we are cold, yet it can also burn and destroy.

Without God's help, taming our tongue is impossible. He even said so. Let's look at James 3:8 (NIV) again.

In verse 8, James tells us "but _____ _____ can tame the _____."

According to verse 9, what does our mouth have the power to do?

_____

_____

_____

What are your thoughts concerning what verse 10 says: "Out of the same mouth come praise and cursing. My brothers, this should not be"?

_____

_____

_____

God desires that we use our tongues to praise Him, and to instruct and bless others. In fact, it's what we are created to do.

In week three, we read Mary's song from Luke 1:46-55. Her beautiful words of praise must have been a sweet aroma to the Lord. Remembering how young she was at the time amazes me! Wouldn't it be wonderful if our words became a sweet aroma of praise to God and encouraged others?

Would the people who know you best say you control your tongue?

In what situations do you find controlling your tongue the most difficult?

- Around family members, especially my children. I say things to them that I deeply regret.

- Around coworkers. They bring out the worst in me.

- Around my girlfriends. We really know how to tear someone apart.

- When stressed. I say things under pressure that I would never say otherwise.

If you desire to build strong healthy friendships, the words you speak are extremely important. There was a woman in my neighborhood who constantly criticized and berated everyone. She was the kind of woman who said, "I simply speak my mind. Let the chips fall where they may." The fact is, most of us already knew our shortcomings and didn't need her to remind us! We were all a work in progress and created in the very image of God. This woman was very lonely. We avoided her at all costs because she made us feel bad about ourselves and put us in a position of defending others.

Over the next few days, pay careful attention to the words you use. Do they encourage? Do they build up? Do they make others feel inspired or better by being in your presence? God's Word says, "For out of the overflow of the heart the mouth speaks" (Matthew 12:34 NIV).

If controlling your tongue is an area in which you struggle, meditate on these two scriptures. When you feel you are about to "lose it," pray these two verses:

Philippians 4:13 NIV: "I can do everything through him who gives me strength."

Psalm 19:14 NIV: "May the words of my mouth and the meditations of my heart be pleasing in your sight."

Below I have included a prayer called "A Blessing for Pleasant Words." I believe it will have a powerful impact on the words you use.

Realizing that words have power, may we use them to encourage others and glorify God. Then we will never again grab our mouths and say…"I can't believe I said that!"

TRAVEL DIARY

Look up the following verses and write their major points in the spaces provided:

Psalm 141:3 _____

Luke 6:25 _____

Ephesians 4:29 _____

TRAVELING MERCIES

A Blessing for Pleasant Words

In the name of Jesus Christ:

Lord, bless me with an understanding of how important it is to set a guard over my mouth, and to keep watch over the words that come from my lips. Father, help me not to speak negative or hurtful words that cause pain and wound spirits.

May I learn quickly that a soft answer turns away wrath and that words thoughtfully spoken bring great rewards. May I express pleasant words, profitable advice, and kindness in all speech and conversations. Lord, may the words of my mouth and the meditations of my heart be pleasing in Your sight.

SNAPSHOT

"The reason we have two ears and only one mouth is that we may hear more and speak less" (Zeno, 333 -264 B.C.).

Women Who Nurture

I hope that you have become as immersed in the lives of these two women as I have. During the many miles we will travel this week, I am going to ask you to combine your imagination with our knowledge of Scripture. I have asked the Holy Spirit to guide us as we tread on the holy ground of God's Word and discover God's calling to women.

Speaking from a woman's point of view, our stopping place this week might be your favorite! Here, we will learn about a gift that God has uniquely placed in women, the gift to *nurture*.

ITINERARY

Day 1–Mighty Women of God

Day 2–The Softer Side of God

Day 3–Calling All Elizabeths

Day 4–Priceless: Seeking Your Elizabeth

⊕ TRAVEL TIP

"Likewise, teach the older women to be reverent in the way they live, not to be slanderers or addicted to much wine, but to teach what is good. Then they can train the younger women to love their husbands and children, to be self-controlled and pure, to be busy at home, to be kind, and to be subject to their husbands so that no one will malign the Word of God" (Titus 2:3 NIV).

WEEK 6, DAY 1
MIGHTY WOMEN OF GOD

SIGHTSEEING, PART 1

During our journey we have spent much time in the first chapter of Luke. Drawing from this Gospel I'd like to share what I imagined took place on that first night at the home of Elizabeth. I pray with all of my heart that it will give you a better understanding of how important women friendships are in the Body of Christ. I'll begin with Mary and later we will hear from Elizabeth.

Climbing into bed, Mary pondered all that had happened in such a short time. During Gabriel's visit, she had longed to ask him more. But, his presence didn't invite more questions—just more faith. When the angel left, she knew what she must do—go to Elizabeth. It was her destiny. Why else would the angel mention her name and that she too was expecting a miracle child? Uncertain of when she would conceive, her instincts told her that it would be soon. She realized she must hurry.

As she journeyed to Elizabeth's, her jumbled thoughts were a constant companion. What would Elizabeth say? Would she believe her? Although she repeatedly reminded herself of Gabriel's words to "fear not," it was difficult. It had taken great faith to make this journey. While she had received the highest honor possible for a woman, her future was uncertain. Yes, there was only one place to go. Who else could possibly understand her circumstances? As she headed to the Judean hills she clung to Gabriel's words, "Your relative Elizabeth is in her sixth month."

Nothing had prepared her for Elizabeth's reaction. Just like Gabriel's visit, another defining moment was engraved upon her heart forever. With Elizabeth's prophetic words she knew that the countdown to the Messiah had begun. Her body would be the dwelling place of God's Son. Suddenly her fear vanished. With the long journey behind her, she pulled the blanket closer and smiled.

For the first time since the angel's appearance, she allowed the honor of being the mother of the Messiah to flood her soul. The fact that God had provided Elizabeth to share this experience with her was another manifestation of His great love. Elated and exhausted, she finally drifted into sleep.

Conversations with Modern-Day "Marys"

Perhaps you are a young woman, and life has suddenly placed you in an overwhelming situation, and you do not know where to turn. This week, we are going to dive into God's Word and learn how God provides for His people. Yes, dear one, God has an Elizabeth for you.

The challenge we have is this: do we have the faith to reach out to *our* Elizabeth? And do we have a teachable heart to receive her instruction and advice?

For each season of life (from youth to midlife and beyond), we need women of faith to nurture and mentor us. Mentors are mature women of faith who are farther down the road of life than we are. They are where we hope to be someday, grounded in faith, established in God's Word, and enjoying life as a believer. These precious women have experienced life and developed a strong faith in God. Now they are equipped to help others navigate successfully through the difficult places of life.

At this young age, Mary had few life experiences that prepared her to be the mother of God's Son and a wife to Joseph. However, there was someone who had a lifetime of experiences—her elderly relative Elizabeth.

Open again turn to Luke 1:56. How long did Mary stay with Elizabeth?

_____

Mary's apprenticeship with Elizabeth would not be brief. Life lessons seldom are. During our study, have you wondered what would have happened if Mary had not gone to Elizabeth's? Briefly write your thoughts.

_____

_____

_____

Today, we are going to do a little more sightseeing before we continue our conversation.

SIGHTSEEING, PART 2

Now, let's imagine the scene from Elizabeth's perspective. Jot your own thoughts in the margin.

Closing the door to the guest room, Elizabeth was too overcome with emotion to sleep. Even though the baby in her womb had finally settled down, she could not! The fact that the mother of the Messiah was sound asleep in the next room still amazed her. She was so consumed with joy that she needed time with her Lord. Once again she spoke the words, "Lord, why am I so favored to have the mother of my Lord come to me?"

Her joy was so much sweeter because of the sorrow she had known. In this sacred moment, her life came full circle. Although she didn't know why, she realized that her painful past would prepare Mary for her unknown future. How like God to use heartache for His glory!

Suddenly she laughed aloud, thinking how Jehovah God had given her a double portion of blessings! *Not only do I have a son in my womb, but for now, a daughter in my home! For as long as the Lord allows, I will treat her like the daughter I never had, the one my heart longed for.*

Elizabeth thought about the wonderful time they would have and made a mental list of all the things she would share with Mary. She would eagerly prepare this young girl for womanhood.

Conversations with Modern-Day "Elizabeths"

I can relate to Elizabeth. I did not have the joy of having a daughter born to me, but I have been privileged to have many spiritual daughters, born out of my heart. They come from every season of life. Yes, my spiritual family is quite large. How about yours? Are you willing to enlarge your family and open your arms to the Marys that God brings your way? Are you willing to equip them to bring Christ into their world?

The call on Elizabeth's life is also our calling, and it is *sacred*. Are you prepared? Do you feel intimidated or inadequate?

Certainly, Elizabeth felt inadequate to mentor the mother of God's Son, but, fortunately for Mary, she didn't let any lack of knowledge stop her. She shared what she knew. Her faith, her love of God, her home, her experience in marriage, her struggles with being the object of scorn and gossip, and the joy that comes from a life of obedience. Now, carefully ponder this: what can you share with the Marys in your world? This week you will discover how you can reach and nurture the younger women God places in your lives. But first, here are a few final thoughts about Mary's time with Elizabeth.

During the next three months, both teacher and student would bond in ways that only women understand. Mary was exactly who Elizabeth needed—she provided youthful energy, companionship, and hope. Elizabeth provided what Mary needed—wisdom, solidity, and hope. In preparing for motherhood, they also prepared for their Messiah.

With holy reverence, they understood that, like Queen Esther, they too were chosen to be a part of God's plan of redemption. What they shared was sacred and planned long before time began. While they could not comprehend it, they chose to cherish it. They were two women who were called by God, for such a time as this. It was friendship, and it was God's idea.

TRAVEL DIARY

Looking back over Elizabeth's life, and drawing from what we have learned, list some things that prepared Elizabeth to be the perfect mentor for Mary:

_____

_____

_____

_____

_____

What qualities might have made Mary a perfect young companion for Elizabeth?

_____

_____

_____

_____

_____

To whom might you be an Elizabeth?

_____

_____

_____

To whom might you be a Mary?

_____

_____

_____

In this study, we view "older" women as Elizabeth and "younger" women as Mary. While physical age certainly applies, it is possible for a younger woman to be "older" in the faith, based on her maturity in Christ. With that in mind, do you think it is possible for a young woman to be an "Elizabeth" or an older woman to be a "Mary?" Write your thoughts here.

_____

_____

_____

 ## TRAVELING MERCIES

Dear Father,
I praise Your holy name for the older women who have invested in me throughout my life. Lord, help me to be a woman who never stops learning. Thank You, Father, for the younger women who bring energy and a fresh perspective on life, serving as a reminder that the cycle of life continues. Amen.

SNAPSHOT

Mentor: someone whose hindsight can become your foresight.

WEEK 6, DAY 2
THE SOFTER SIDE OF GOD

SIGHTSEEING

You may recall an innovative marketing campaign several years ago when Sears wanted to expand their image to show that they were not just a store for tools and sporting equipment, but were also a great source of fashionable apparel for women. Commercials ran showing "the softer side of Sears" with women saying such things as, "I came in for a Die Hard and left with an outfit to die for."

Today, we are going to explore the "softer side of God." To do so, I'd like you to look at a few Scriptures that reveal this dimension of our Father from both the Old and New Testament. Please turn to the following verses: Matthew 23:37; Isaiah 49:15-16; Isaiah 66:13; and Zephaniah 3:17.

Do you see how the word "nurture" can be applied to the characteristics you saw in these verses? Webster defines "nurture" as:

1. **"To take care of a young thing:** to give tender care and protection to a young child, animal or plant, helping it to grow and develop

2. **To encourage someone or something to flourish:** to encourage somebody or something to grow, develop, thrive, and be successful."

What's the first thought that comes to your mind when you hear the word "nurture"?

My first thought is to picture a mother cradling her baby. Tenderly she feeds, protects, and cares for her baby's needs.

I remember when I became a new grandma. What a joy it was to observe the way my daughter-in-law, Heather, provided for my granddaughter's needs. While it's very demanding and time-consuming, the investment is priceless. In addition to her basic needs, Madison will need to know that she has value and significance. She will need affirmation, encouragement, and unconditional love.

As her Nana, I have the privilege of contributing and helping to fulfill those needs, so that Madison can become the woman God created her to be. I look forward to this calling with great excitement. Nurturing others is a woman's specialty.

In His wonderful and divine creation, God created women to be His softer side. We have numerous talents, abilities, strengths, and leadership skills. Yet it is our softer side that makes us unique. Certainly, some men can be tender, but that's the exception. For most women, it comes naturally. God designed us that way. It's actually a "right-brain" activity. Most people think primarily with the left side of their brain, but women have the ability to work with both. That is why we multi-task so well.

Studies have shown that female infants recognize and respond to human faces more quickly than male infants. Male babies tend to respond more quickly to objects. Give a preschool girl a crayon and paper, and she will likely draw pictures of people. A preschool boy, however, will draw objects such as cars, trucks, and boats. Interesting!

This tendency goes back to the beginning of time. When God created Adam, the first thing Adam saw was God, and the second was the garden. Worship God, tend the garden. The first thing Eve saw was God, then Adam. Worship God, tend to Adam. I laugh when I share this with you. Since that time, man has been trying to "fix things" and woman has been trying to "fix her man!"

Both genders are fearfully and wonderfully made and created in the image of God. But, we are different. Let's embrace those differences and enjoy what we were created to represent—the softer side of our Lord.

CONVERSATIONS

We realize that nurturing a young child is essential in helping him/her develop into a healthy adult, but did you realize that friendships need nurturing, too? Here's why:

A big concern of Christian women is the epidemic of shallow relationships among women. In an age when broken marriages, moral decline, and unbelievable heartache are frighteningly high, our God-given support system is lacking.

What happened? Why do we know more people than ever before, yet know very little about each other? Why do we know more about the latest celebrity break-up yet very little about the young woman in our Sunday school class going through her own divorce?

Unfortunately, we live in Hurryville. Hurry and get the kids to school. Hurry and get to work. Hurry to Bible study. Hurry to the ball field. Hurry. Hurry. Hurry. In this "hurry up, see you later" world we don't take the time to invest in relationships like the generations before us did. Our busy lives leave very little time to invest in meaningful relationships. Take a look at the "then" and "now":

Then	Now
Sit on the porch and visit with neighbors.	Wave to a neighbor while rushing off to do errands.
Gather for Sunday dinners in homes.	Rush out of church to beat the crowd to the restaurant.
Play outside, pretending and imagining.	Sign up for several structured activities.
Ride bikes and take long walks with friends.	Drive alone to the gym to workout with strangers.
Enjoy long chats over a glass of tea.	Send a quick text message or an e-mail.

How about you and me changing this tendency in our circle of influence by adjusting our schedules and our priorities? Let's take care of our friendships as the nurturing women God designed us to be.

 TRAVEL DIARY

Realizing that God created us for friendships, let's look at how women in the body of Christ can nurture our relationships. We'll use Elizabeth as a perfect example.

Scripture doesn't allow us to know exactly what took place during Mary's three-month visit at Elizabeth's home. However, the Lord has given us the wonderful gift of imagination. When we combine that gift with our own life experiences and what we know of the Jewish culture, perhaps we can picture what took place.

Referring back to Webster's definition of "nurture," how do you think Elizabeth nurtured Mary?

To Take Care of a Young Thing …

What kind of care would Mary, an unwed, pregnant, Jewish girl need?

How do you think Elizabeth provided for that need?

_____

_____

_____

What may have been some of the tender moments that these two women enjoyed?

_____

_____

_____

To Protect ...

It is doubtful that anyone knew that Mary was pregnant with the coming Messiah, so she didn't need immediate protection from public scandal or punishment. However, Elizabeth did protect her secret.

In what other ways might Elizabeth have protected Mary?

_____

_____

_____

For an unmarried girl expecting the Messiah, I would think she might need protection from self-doubt and fear. Is there someone you know who might need this kind of protection?

_____

_____

_____

To Encourage ...

How do you think Elizabeth encouraged Mary so that she could flourish as a wife and mother and into a mighty woman of God?

_____

_____

_____

Did you know there are Marys in your world? Some of them sit in your church pews on Sunday morning. Their backgrounds vary. Some have recently transferred from another area due to their husband's career. Others are single moms trying to rebuild their lives. Others may have returned to church after a long absence, giving church another chance. Some are new to church and may feel intimidated. All of these women need someone to nurture them in the Body of Christ. God has placed us there to meet that need. If we accept God's call to be an "Elizabeth" in the life of a "Mary," let's look to Elizabeth to be our example.

For a short season, Elizabeth poured her life into a young woman who needed a best friend and a mentor. Mary eventually left Elizabeth's home to become the woman, mother, and wife she was meant to be. I'm sure this goodbye was bittersweet for Elizabeth. This will be true with some of our friends too. We must invest in others without expecting something back, and be willing to let go and trust God to fulfill our emotional needs.

The following is a short inventory designed to help you take a good look at your current lifestyle and schedule as it relates to nurturing others. After each question, also ask yourself, "What would Elizabeth do?"

Who are the Marys in my circle of influence and how can I reach out to them.

Is there someone new in church who I should invite to Bible study?

_____

Is there a woman in my church who is going through a difficult time and could use a phone call or card?

_____

Is there a first-time mom in my church who could use a visit or a meal (maybe weeks or months after the initial provisions of the first few weeks)?

_____

Is there a new coworker who looks as if she could use a friend?

_____

When was the last time I sent a note to a friend?

_____

In the last month, how often did I make time to simply enjoy a friendship? Once a week? _____ A couple of times? _____ Not at all? _____

Today would be a perfect day to show someone that you care. God has uniquely gifted you—share your gift with someone today!

Traveling Mercies

Dear Father,
I am busy, not always with unimportant things, but busy with the responsibilities of life. I ask that You help me to slow down and take an inventory of my activities so that I can spend more time nurturing and enjoying the precious relationships in my life. Lord, help me to become a woman like Elizabeth, who graciously opened her home and invested in someone who needed a dear friend. Amen.

Snapshot

"Good friendships are fragile things and require as much care as any other fragile and precious thing." (Randolph Bourne, American Author)

Travel Advisory

> If you spend time and invest in a woman and things don't turn out as you hoped, trust God. We are responsible to fulfill our calling, and He alone is responsible for the results.

WEEK 6, DAY 3
CALLING ALL ELIZABETHS

If you are a young woman (under age 35), please still read today's devotion, so that you will understand that God loved you so much that He designed a marvelous plan to help you succeed abundantly. His plan was to place in your life godly, experienced women who could help you navigate through life more easily. God always provides for His people. Tomorrow's lesson will focus on the younger women in the body of Christ.

SIGHTSEEING

Scripture reading: Titus 2:1-5

I love being around godly women. They provide a sense of security that allows me to be myself, and encourages me to want to become more.

You may find this hard to believe, but we will never outgrow our need for the Body of Christ. As believers, we will continue to need both instruction and encouragement to reach our full potential in Christ. Without our sisters in the faith that would be impossible.

In today's culture, we often turn to every source for advice and answers, except those mighty women of faith that God has placed in our lives.

We must never forget the powerful, but subtle, influence the media has. In my younger years, celebrity, and media had a huge impact on me, though I was a "church girl," a believer since childhood. Still, the desire to look like and be like the latest celebrity dictated many of my decisions.

Recalling my struggles as a young wife and mother, it wasn't celebrities or talk shows that had the right answers. It was godly, mature women of faith—women who were in the Word and living it. These gracious women that God placed into my life had a relationship with the Lord and were willing to invest in a young woman like me. I am convinced that God gave them an extra measure of grace where I was concerned and "I'm mighty beholden" to them. These women were the epitome of today's scripture.

Until I became a student of the Word, I didn't know about this passage in Titus, or that God had called the older women to train younger women. And training was just what I needed. Not from celebrities, talk shows, or even my husband, but from godly women who understood the challenges of womanhood.

Now it's our turn. We are the "Titus Two" women and the "Elizabeths" of the 21st century. The need is great.

CONVERSATIONS

But, why the need?

So that you may fully understand the importance of our calling to minister to younger women, I am providing some background information on our scripture passage. If time allows, please read the first and second chapter of Titus. However, we will focus on Titus 2:1-5.

Paul had left Titus to organize the church in Crete, and it was a huge responsibility. The Cretans were a pagan culture, desperately in need of godly instructions. They were receiving the message of salvation but knew nothing concerning God's principles of conduct for followers of Christ. Even their own prophets said the Cretans were always "liars, evil brutes, and lazy gluttons" (Titus 1:12). Paul gave Titus specific instructions on how to succeed at organizing the church. It required help from older men and women who were well established in faith.

Like the unchurched people in Crete, our communities are full of women who are unchurched and know very little about God. Some may have attended church as a child, but have no grasp of the saving knowledge Christ offers or what it means to have a personal relationship with Him. There are others who have never had the joy or privilege of being in church, and have no idea that God has a divine purpose for their lives.

These are the women in our world. They need nurturing and instruction from godly women. God has called you for that purpose. From the beginning of this study, my heart's desire was for you to know that God ordained friendship. It provides the perfect environment to reach others for Christ. When friendship is established, then you have the opportunity to influence the next generation to know and serve God.

First, let's understand exactly what our calling is. Thankfully God has provided the perfect curriculum in Titus 2:1-5. Let's go there now. Please read it carefully and engrave it upon your heart.

Verse 3 (NIV), says we are to be "… reverent in the way we live, not to be slanderers, or addicted to much wine, but to teach what is good." Then we can train the younger women. Not until we have met these standards can we instruct the younger women. To be an effective teacher or witness for Christ, we must live by example. We must be "doers of the word" ourselves (James 1:22).

Looking at verses 4-5, list below what the older women are to teach the younger women:

_____

_____

_____

Now, let's take each one and determine why younger women would need to learn these specific characteristics for a lifestyle of godliness. Also evaluate yourself to see if you are living the "Titus Two" scripture. Determine any areas that you need to work on.

1. Why would younger women need instructions on how to "love" their husbands and children?

_____

_____

_____

Love is not a feeling, is it? Love must be put into action and demonstrated. Today we live in a very self-absorbed society that lives by the motto, "It's all about me." It's not unusual for people to want a relationship so they can "be happy" or find the person "who satisfies me." Sometimes women live vicariously through their children or a successful husband. Teaching others what love really means is a tremendous calling, but it defines who we are and who God is. In fact, God called it His greatest commandment.

2. Why self-control?

_____

_____

_____

In Galatians 5:23, self-control is listed as a fruit of the Spirit. Personally, I believe it is one of the most difficult to achieve. However I know that the only person we really control is ourselves.

3. Why purity?

_____

_____

_____

I have never seen a more desperate time for women to understand God's definition of purity. The world sends messages that are completely contrary to God's Word and degrade women. I believe that when a woman understands God's definition of purity, she is set free.

4. Why should we be busy at home?

_____

_____

_____

Home should be the safe place for our families—a refuge. To maintain a safe, loving, orderly, and comfortable home is one of the best gifts a woman can give her family. Many women also contribute to the home by earning a living. Young women today need encouragement on effectively juggling these roles and priorities.

5. Why should we be kind?

_____

_____

_____

Kindness doesn't come naturally or easily. It's a choice we make. But, over time, when we implement something, it becomes a lifestyle. Be kind, beloved.

6. Finally, and perhaps most controversial of all, is for women to be "subject" to their husbands.

_____

_____

_____

Making the decision to obey and accept God's instructions concerning this matter was one of the best things I did for myself and my family. I realized that God loved me, and that He would take care of me. If my husband failed in his position as leader in our home, he was under God's authority. I belonged to God, and He would intervene. I also realized I had a huge responsibility in praying for my husband as the leader in our home. (Just to give you hope, the leader in our home—my sweet husband—just made pancakes for my breakfast. Ahhh …God is so good!)

At the end of verse 5, Paul explains why this type of conduct is necessary for followers of Christ:

"So that no one will

_____   _____   _____   _____   _____ .

To malign means to "slander, hurt, smear, damage, and criticize." Never do we want to malign the gospel of Jesus Christ! However, when we don't model the standard God has designed for believers, that is exactly what we do.

The younger women in your life were handpicked by God. He has given you a wonderful opportunity and a high calling to invest in the lives of others. God knows that He can trust you with this assignment!

 ## Travel Diary

Who are the younger women in your life who need godly training?

_____

_____

What is the best way to train younger women? What are some obstacles? (time, feel inadequate, don't know how to begin, etc.)

_____

_____

How can you overcome any obstacle that prevents you from fulfilling God's call?

_____

_____

Does your church have a mentoring program? If yes, are you involved?

_____

_____

If not, would you be willing to pray about how to begin one?

_____

_____

What are some life lessons you would like to pass on to the women in your circle of influence? Briefly write them down:

_____

_____

Dear one, are you ready for this assignment? Earnestly seek God's help in preparing for and fulfilling your call. The need is great!

TRAVELING MERCIES

Dear Father,
I praise You and thank You for every godly woman who encouraged
me during my life's journey. Now I realize that it is my turn. Please

equip me, give me knowledge and understanding of Your word so that I can complete this assignment. I understand the need and accept the responsibility. Help me to conduct myself in a manner worthy of the Gospel of Jesus Christ, a living example of the Titus 2 Scripture. Amen.

SNAPSHOT

At the heart of the nurturing process is a genuine concern for others.

TRAVEL TIP

I truly wish that every church had a mentoring program in place. We are greatly in need of men and women in the Body of Christ to step forward and accept this responsibility. Thankfully, there are some wonderful books and programs to help churches implement a mentoring program. Here are two of my favorites:

A Woman's High Calling—Ten Essentials for Godly Living by Elizabeth George, and *Woman to Woman* by Janet Thompson (for church ministry). Her program has guidelines for both the mentor and the person being mentored, which helps the relationship succeed.

Week 6, Day 4
Priceless: Seek Your Elizabeth

🚌 Sightseeing

Would you like to treat yourself to something special, something refreshing that will renew your soul? I have the perfect solution…a day with a godly older woman.

That's right. I recommend that you do lunch, and make it a long one. However, I must attach a disclaimer. It will be habit forming!

If you're thinking, "That sounds great, Frankie, but where do I find someone like that?" Just keep reading, girlfriend! God's Word never fails. Let's go back to Titus 2:2-5 and Luke 1:39.

In God's divine and unique way of helping us to enjoy a life in Christ, God specifically called the older women in the church to show us how. But so often we fail to take advantage of this. Most churches are filled with godly women who are willing to offer friendship and to nurture younger women in their faith journey. These mighty women of faith are well equipped to help young women navigate through life. They've been there, done that, and have the experience to prove it!

Like Mary, there are times in our lives when we desperately need the love and wisdom of a godly older woman. Even those of us blessed with a godly mother sometimes need another perspective. Based upon the Scriptures Luke recorded as Mary's song, we can be fairly confident that she had a godly mother. But for this particular time, she needed a woman who understood her unique circumstances. That woman was Elizabeth, a woman like herself who was also experiencing a miraculous pregnancy. No matter how many life experiences Mary's mother had, that wasn't one of them! Notice that in Luke, we see that Mary went to Elizabeth, not the other way around. Grab that lesson my friend! "Mary got ready and hurried to the hill country of Judea."

🕐 Conversations

Are you in need of an Elizabeth? I am! Even now as I begin my exciting journey as a grandma, I still need an Elizabeth in my own life, someone who has already been where I must go. I continually seek the company of women much older because we never outgrow our need to be nurtured and encouraged.

Are you at a place where you need strength for your faith journey? Perhaps an older woman in your church would be thrilled to have *you* as a friend. Would you please take the initiative? You will be amazed at the priceless gift that awaits you when spending time with an older woman who has walked with the Savior for many years. That lovely woman in the blue suit in your church pew has a history with God and a life to prove it. Take a chance my friend, reach out to her. Your Elizabeth is waiting.

 ## TRAVEL DIARY

Mary's heart was ready to learn and receive from Elizabeth. During this week, prepare your heart to seek your Elizabeth by answering these questions with complete honesty:

Where do I turn for advice?

_____ Family _____ Girlfriends _____ Husband _____Talk show/media

_____ Self-help books _____ God's Word

Do the media and celebrities have a major influence on you? _____

Who are your role models? (Before you answer, think carefully. When we model the behavior of others, they become our role models.)

_____

_____

_____

_____

_____

Did you know that the people whom we associate with, the movies we watch, and the books we read influence us? _____

Before reading today's lesson, did you know that God had specifically called older women to instruct younger women? _____

Why do you think God planned it that way?

_____

_____

_____

From our scripture in Titus, list what the older women are to teach the younger women to be:

_____   _____

_____   _____

_____   _____

Which one of these would be the hardest for you to implement in your daily life?

_____

Why? _____

_____

Could you use some guidance in some of these areas? _____

The first step is to pray, and then ask yourself, "Do I have a teachable heart?" _____

"Am I open to instruction?" _____

"Am I willing to listen and apply the instructions that my mentor recommends?" _____

If you answered yes, please read and apply the Travel Tips below. Then believe God will send you an Elizabeth.

 ## Traveling Mercies

Dear Father,
Thank You for providing godly women who have a heart for You to lead and guide me in my faith journey. Help me to find someone who can relate to me and instruct me on how to be more like Jesus. Father, help me to have a teachable heart so that I will become the woman that You created me to be. Amen.

 ## Snapshot

"Blessed is the influence of one true, loving human soul on another" (George Eliot, English Novelist 1819-1880).

Travel Tip

How to Find an Elizabeth
Pray and ask God to lead you to an Elizabeth. God knows your heart like no one else. He knows what you need. Mary sought her mentor, but received a strong recommendation from Gabriel. Therefore, seek God and be wise in selecting your mentor.

Get involved with a Bible study where older women are teaching. Just by listening to them, you can learn so much about life and godliness. Possibly, you may find a woman with whom you feel a kindred spirit who you can invite to have coffee or lunch.

Engage in some activity where you can interact with older women in your church. Seek out the company of older women and let the relationship(s) evolve. Don't be afraid to ask if you can join in an activity with an "older women's group" (at some churches they are called "circles"). You can learn a lot about life just by hanging out with older women, and many of them are a hoot!

Visit the Christian bookstore for books by older women. There are a number of older women who have put their godly wisdom and experience in writing. Start with a basic and simple-to-understand Bible study, or choose an author who has had success in an area of current interest: child rearing, marriage, divorce, money management, or dealing with teenagers. The knowledge is out there, so grab it!

If you find yourself in a desperate situation, call your pastor and ask him to recommend someone.

Once you begin to establish a relationship, remember to respect her time and not abuse the new friendship. Take a moment to read the following guidelines so that you can enjoy a relationship that will have long-term effects.

BONUS MILES

What a Mentor Is (from *Woman to Woman* by Janet Thompson):

In her book, *Woman to Woman,* Janet Thompson outlines some thoughts about what a mentor is and is not. While the role of mentor is a very important one, the relationship should also have healthy boundaries. Janet says that mentors are godly women willing to step up to the privilege of sharing life experiences with younger women. She is an example of what a woman following Christ looks like. A mentor is different from a role model in that she takes a personal interest in your life and interacts with you. This relationship is built around the Lord and His Word. While she can advise you, you should not expect her to make choices for you, or solve your problems. Mentors are not professional counselors or available 24-7. Mary stayed with Elizabeth for three months, learning all she could, and then she moved on and began her life.

Women Who Delight

I am amazed this is the last week of our journey. I pray you have had a delightful time exploring God's Word and learning the importance He places on
friendships. The places we visit in Scripture this week are quite intriguing
and will provide life-changing knowledge for believers.

In fact, we'll learn something we should never forget: God delights in us and
He's crazy about you! We'll visit with Mary and Elizabeth a bit more and even
Zachariah will join us, reminding us how gracious our God is. So let's get going,
girlfriend. Delightful Drive is just ahead and it's going to be…well…delightful!

ITINERARY

Day 1–Delightful Moments to Come

Day 2–Delightful Moments with Others

Day 3–Delighting in God's Word

Day 4–Delighting in God My Father

✦ TRAVEL TIP

*"Surely then you will find delight in the Almighty and will lift up your
face to God"* (Job 22:26 NIV).

WEEK 7, DAY 1
DELIGHTFUL MOMENTS TO COME

SIGHTSEEING

Our Scripture reading is Revelation 21:1-6. In February 2007 it became very special to me. I especially found verse 4 to be a dwelling place for my spirit. It says, "He will wipe every tear from their eyes. There will be no more death or mourning or crying or pain, for the old order of things has passed away" (NIV).

I am what many would call a "blessed" woman. I've enjoyed good health, a fairy-tale marriage of over 35 years, a godly son, an adorable grandchild, a job that I love, and wonderful friends who I wouldn't trade for anything. However, in the blink of an eye, life can change; and mine did.

One afternoon I was in my office writing a message for an upcoming women's retreat. My schedule was packed with speaking engagements, and I would be traveling all over the country in the coming weeks.

As I moved along in my preparation, I began to feel the symptoms of a bladder infection. Bummer! I'd dealt with these for years and didn't worry about them much. But I didn't like how they depleted my energy. I didn't have time to be sick!

As usual, my doctor prescribed an antibiotic. Unfortunately, this particular bacteria was much stronger than the prescribed medication could handle. Several days later, I found myself in the hospital suffering from renal failure! My kidneys were functioning at only four percent.

For the first time in my life, I would travel to a place I had never been before, to the valley of serious illness. I'd been to the valley of heartbreak, loneliness and loss, but not here. I was completely at the mercy of others.

After days of the best medical care, my kidneys remained shut down. To hydrate me, my doctors flushed me so fast that the fluids spilled over into my heart and lungs. Therefore, I could hardly breathe without the help of oxygen.

Later, the doctor informed us since there was no improvement for such a long time, I would need either dialysis or a transplant.

What? Dialysis or a transplant? Those words rocked my world. This was a bladder infection! I'd had them since I was twenty years old. Now the doctor was talking transplant or dialysis! When he left the room, my hope followed. If my future meant either of those options, life as I knew it would change drastically.

I feared how I would handle that. I didn't lose my faith, but I did lose my desire to fight.

Because I am a believer in Christ Jesus, I began to think about heaven. I'd loved Jesus since I was a child in Vacation Bible School and always looked forward to living in heaven. So, I began to dwell on the scriptures in Revelations 21. They were my comfort.

However in spite of the joy that heaven inspired, reality set in. I thought about the things that I would not get to do. I wondered as any servant would, was my work complete? Had I done enough? Without question, our salvation cannot be earned, but James also tells us that "… faith without works is useless" (James 2:20 NASB). I had served out of devotion not duty. Still I wanted to have my "to do" list complete when I stood before Him! I pictured myself with a smile on my face saying, "Mission complete, Father!"

Then I thought about the people whom I loved so much and their continuing life without me. I knew how difficult that would be for me if I were in their place. So, I wept. But I also knew that someday I would see them again. Then, I began to prepare myself for my road trip home to heaven.

The first thing I did was to ask the Lord to help me do an inventory of my heart to see if there were areas that needed confessing or cleansing. I knew the blood of Christ had redeemed me and what Christ did on the cross made it possible for me to appear before God as a forgiven child. His Word said so, and I believed Him. In His tender mercy He showed me that I was forgiven and that heaven awaited me.

That's not to say that if I had my life to live over again, there wouldn't be any "do overs." Unfortunately, I have made numerous mistakes and committed sins that grieve my spirit and cause me deep regret. I am living proof of the scripture that says, "For all have sinned and fall short of the glory of God" (Romans 3:23 NIV).

In the dark of the night I quietly surrendered my fate to Him. He knew the desires of my heart and the plans that He had for me. All of my days were ordained by Him. To close my eyes on earth for the last time was to open them in heaven. Yes, I was ready to face God. Actually, I couldn't wait.

CONVERSATIONS

Before I tell you the rest of the story, I want to ask you a question.

If you were lying in a hospital bed, knowing that you could be facing your last days on earth, what would run through your mind?

Do you think you could come to the point of being ready to meet God?

Beloved, let me encourage you to be ready for that day. I've shared this earlier, but allow me to reiterate—God's grace is available to you! Simply accept it! Christ did the work on the cross and offers you His gift of salvation.

Now, to finish the story ...

The next morning, I was physically worse. My mother and a dear friend came to anoint me with oil and pray healing scriptures over me. A prayer chain of women began across the country. Some were face down crying out to God on my behalf.

Three hours later, I experienced the divine healing of Jesus Christ my Savior. It wasn't immediate, but I slowly began to leave the valley of illness and pull out of renal failure. Where there had been darkness, light began to glow. My healing was so miraculous that even with the extreme attack to my kidneys, I would not need dialysis or a transplant! Blessed be the Lord who "heals all your diseases" (Psalm 103:3b NIV).

I cannot explain why God chose to heal me, or why I was spared the process of going on a transplant list or having to receive dialysis. No one can ever explain God. But this I know, when I was at my sickest point, doctors and family could provide only some level of physical comfort. But I needed an *inner* comfort. The kind only God provides. And, He did!

Even though it was the most horrible time I have ever experienced, it was one of the holiest and most beautiful moments of my life. It has enabled me to speak with boldness and assurance that He is Lord.

TRAVEL DIARY

Looking at today's scripture (Revelation 21:1-6), list the delightful moments waiting for us in heaven:

_____

_____

_____

All of the promises in the passage are spectacular, but go back and circle the one that means the most to you. Mine is "no more death." I look forward to never attending another funeral or saying "goodbye" to a loved one.

How does knowing all that awaits us in heaven make you feel?

_____

_____

_____

Does this knowledge provide strength to help you move forward?

_____

_____

_____

When John wrote Revelation, he had been exiled to the Isle of Patmos. Some report that he was elderly (perhaps around 90) and had suffered much for Christ. Revelation was written when Christians were entering a time of persecution. John wanted them, and us, to stand firm and stay focused on eternity.

Can you do that? We are living in difficult times, but let's remember that God is with us, but, in heaven, *we* will be with Him! Now that is something that we can delight in!

Until that time, how can you delight in your relationship with the Lord?

_____

_____

_____

Think about seeing Jesus face to face and Him dwelling among us in a visible way. Wouldn't you like to be ready to meet Him having enjoyed and delighted in a vibrant relationship with Him while on earth?

One way to enjoy this is to stay in full communication with God, not allowing sin to invade your life and block this fellowship.

Have you done an inventory recently asking God to point out areas that need confessing and cleansing? Is there anyone you need to forgive?

Is there anyone you need to ask forgiveness from?

Remember, life can change quickly. Be ready, girlfriend. Don't waste another moment.

TRAVELING MERCIES

Father God,
We delight in the fact that someday, we will be with You. When that
day comes, there will be no more death, mourning, or pain, and You,
heavenly Father, will wipe away every tear with Your holy hand!
Until that time comes, help us delight in You and in the joy that our
salvation brings. Amen.

SNAPSHOT

"As a doctor, I know when my work has ended and God's work must begin" (Brian Weirick, MD, my medical doctor).

WEEK 7, DAY 2
DELIGHTFUL MOMENTS WITH OTHERS

SIGHTSEEING

Few things provide more pleasure than spending "fun time" with my girlfriends. I love those moments when we let our hair down and just enjoy being women. I have a wide variety of friends: some are young, some are right in the throes of motherhood, others are my age, and others are enjoying the golden years of life. Each of them makes my life better in her own unique way. Many of them have been walking with the Lord a long time, and are secure in His love. Their maturity in Christ provides a freedom that allows us to enjoy true friendship on a deeper level.

Their maturity and freedom in Christ allows them to rejoice and celebrate those moments when God smiles down on *me* without wondering why He didn't do the same particular thing for them. They are simply so excited and happy for me. So, what happens when it *is* their *turn*? When God smiles down on them? How should I react?

What prevents us from delighting when it's our friend's turn? That's what we'll talk about today. But first, I'd like to share a moment when God opened heaven and poured down a blessing on my life.

It was my husband Wayland's birthday, and I had invited our only son Andy and his wife Heather over for dinner. Those two are very clever and creative when it comes to birthday surprises, but on this particular birthday, they outdid themselves.

Before sitting down to the table, my son handed his dad a birthday card. That should have been my first clue that something was up, because we always open gifts *after* the meal—that's tradition!

When Wayland opened the card, he began to jump up and down like a young child at Christmas. In fact, he started doing some dance moves that even John Travolta couldn't emulate! That is *so* out of character for him. He is a man of few words, much less dancing! His favorite TV channel is the History Channel! Get my drift?

I was so shocked by his enthusiasm that I jumped up to see what the fuss was about. He shoved the card toward me and said, "Read the card! Read the card!" The card said, "Happiness is having a grandpa like you." What? He's not a grandpa!

Then I saw the signature: "Love, Andy, Heather and Baby Sherman." Woo Hoo! Wayland was going to be a grandpa. And if Wayland was going to be a grandpa, that meant I …would be a grandma!

It is impossible to fully express the delightful moment our household enjoyed that cold January night. We didn't just celebrate a birthday but the upcoming birth of the new life that would be joining our family.

After Andy and Heather left and the "birthday boy" went to bed, guess what I did? I called my two best friends. I couldn't wait to share the wonderful news. They were grandmothers already, and they screamed in delight for my joy.

That's why we need girlfriends, beloved—to share the delightful moments when God pours out His blessings!

We can only imagine the delightful moments experienced by Elizabeth and Mary. Just think—way before the age of technology, they knew the gender of their baby before he came. Almighty God had already named their sons. These two expectant mothers with two separate callings could celebrate and rejoice in each other's joy.

God desires that we also share our delightful moments. Sadly, though, we sometimes miss out on the joy of this experience. So, pour yourself a cup of coffee and let's sit down and talk this one through.

🔅 CONVERSATIONS

What keeps us from fully rejoicing when God smiles down on a girlfriend? The biggest obstacle is that green-eyed monster called jealousy. It doesn't take much to feed this monster, and as you feed him, he will grow.

We've all felt jealousy toward another person at some point in our life. It's human nature. But have you thought of the fact that jealousy is actually rooted in another major challenge? That's right. It's rooted in fear. It's the fear that we can be replaced. This fear can destroy relationships faster than anything else. Women become jealous when they feel threatened. When we feel insecure about our looks, our talents, our abilities, or any number of other things, it can bring out the worst in us. Because of our need for intimacy and acceptance, we tend to attack if the least bit threatened. As followers of Christ, we cannot do that. Instead, we must follow the example of Elizabeth. We must realize our calling, and know that God has specific plans for us that no one else could or should fulfill.

 ## TRAVEL DIARY

Let's look at the first chapter of Luke and note some of the similarities and differences of Mary and Elizabeth:

Similarities   Differences

_____   _____

_____   _____

_____   _____

_____   _____

Of course, we can't help but point out the age difference but I don't want us to miss the most profound difference. Elizabeth was expecting a son. Mary was expecting the Messiah. Remember, Elizabeth referred to Mary as "the mother of her Lord" (v. 43).

Not one hint of jealousy appears in the heart of this elderly woman who had experienced years of heartache and disappointment. She knew how to celebrate and delight in the moments when God blessed her loved ones.

How about you? Do you struggle with twinges of jealousy? I do! When I feel the old green-eyed monster starting to grow, I run to my heavenly Father and tell Him! If not, the monster grows and completely takes over.

Where are you in your spiritual journey of becoming mature in Christ? Is there anything holding you back? One way to tell is to gauge how you react when a friend receives a blessing that perhaps *you* have been praying for (a pregnancy, financial blessing, a new house, job promotion).

When a friend receives a blessing, how do you react?

_____ Delighted

_____ Bitter

_____ Cool

_____ Resentful toward her and God

_____ Other

Elizabeth understood that she was to be the mother of the forerunner to the Messiah. She determined to fill that role with joy and excellence. I believe that deep in her heart she would prove herself worthy of her calling. Never would she be jealous that Mary was the one chosen to be the mother of the Messiah. I wonder if I could be that humble.

Isn't it amazing that Elizabeth called Mary "blessed among women" (v.42)? Do you express terms of endearment and compliments to your friends even when things are difficult for you or when the blessings of their calling differ from yours? My friend, it is time to do this.

I believe that all of us have dealt with jealousy. The difference is what we do with that temptation as soon as it reveals itself. When we allow the Lord to fill our hearts, and trust Him for the outcomes of our lives, then we can give to our friends out of His abundance. Then, not only can we call our girlfriends when great things happen to us, we can cheer when wonderful things happen to them!

TRAVELING MERCIES

Dear Father,
Help me to be a mature woman in Christ who delights in moments of joy, not only in my life, but in the lives of others. When I feel twinges of jealousy, help me run to You who knows my every need. Precious Lord, help me to know my calling and to understand that it is unique. Then I can experience the true delight and contentment that comes from serving You. Amen.

SNAPSHOT

I will choose to be joyful and not jealous when God blesses my girlfriends.

TRAVEL NOTE

Madison Patrice Sherman was born on September 15, 2005. What a delight she is!

Week 7, Day 3
Delighting in God's Word

Sightseeing & Conversations

During our sightseeing today, we will again combine both Scripture and imagination. By now you can tell that my background is in the arts. In fact some have labeled me a DQ—drama queen. Hopefully it has enhanced our study! Today we will expand the scope of our thinking to include Zechariah. I will use scriptures and interact with my own comments, much like you'd experience watching a drama. Therefore, for today, our sightseeing and conversations will be combined.

While Mary stayed at Elizabeth's home, every morning began with the reciting of the Shema.

> Hear, O Israel: The LORD our God, the LORD is one. Love the LORD your God with all your heart and with all your soul and with all your strength. These commandments that I give you today are to be upon your hearts. Impress them on your children. Talk about them when you sit at home and when you walk along the road, when you lie down and when you get up. Tie them as symbols on your hands and bind them on your foreheads. Write them on the doorframes of your houses and on your gates. (Deuteronomy 6:4-9 NIV)

It was Jewish tradition to recite this passage before a light breakfast and daily responsibilities. However, today was different. This was the day Zechariah would finally share with Mary all that happened on the day he was chosen to serve in the temple. She had wondered if the angel's visitation to him had been anything like her experience.

As Elizabeth and Mary waited eagerly at the table, the old priest brought in several large scrolls. He handled them with meticulous care and placed them in specific order. Since he was unable to speak, Elizabeth would have the honor of reciting the words.

With sacred trust Zechariah handed Elizabeth the scroll and pointed to the place where she should begin.

"Amazing," she thought. "This is the exact Scripture we were reading from the morning Zechariah left to go and serve at the temple. We'd been praying for the coming Messiah that very day, but never dreamed the mother of the Messiah would be in our home a few months later!"

All three stood as Elizabeth read the holy Word of God. It was the first time either of them had heard a woman read from the prophet Isaiah. She read with reverence: "Therefore the Lord himself will give you a sign: the virgin will be with child and give birth to a son, and will call him Immanuel" (Isaiah 7:14 NIV). Elizabeth smiled at Mary and then continued in Isaiah 9:6, this time her voice resonating with power and assurance!

> For unto us a child is born, to us a son is given, and the government will be on his shoulders and he will be called Wonderful Counselor, Mighty God, Everlasting Father, Prince of Peace. Of the increase of his government and peace there will be no end. He will reign on David's throne and over his kingdom, establishing and upholding it with justice and righteousness from that time on and forever. The zeal of the Lord Almighty will accomplish this.

By now, Mary and the old priest had lost their composure. The only sounds in the room were those of weeping.

Wiping his eyes, the old priest took out another scroll. This time it was recorded by him. From his youth Zechariah had been one to put everything in writing, never realizing this childhood habit would have a profound effect on history. Before leaving the temple, the stunned priest had carefully penned every word the angel had spoken moments after his departure. Today, Mary would hear them for the first time.

This time, Mary would perform the reading of the word. There was another life to celebrate and his parents were long-time followers of Yahweh. Before she began, Zechariah took Elizabeth's hand and placed his other gently on her belly where his baby grew.

With a maturity far beyond her years, Mary read:

"Alone in the holy place I began my sacred duties, scattering incenses on the golden altar like thousands of priests before me. I was completely captivated by a moment I had longed for all of my life. I was deep in prayer, I sensed a presence. Was it the presence of Yahweh? Then I heard his voice:"

> "Do not be afraid, Zechariah; your prayer has been heard. Your wife Elizabeth will bear you a son, and you are to give him the name John.

He will be a joy and delight to you, and many will rejoice because of his birth, for he will be great in the sight of the Lord. He is never to take wine or other fermented drink, and he will be filled with the Holy Spirit even from birth. Many of the people of Israel will he bring back to the Lord their God. And he will go on before the Lord, in the spirit and power of Elijah, to turn the hearts of the fathers to their children and the disobedient to the wisdom of the righteous—to make ready a people prepared for the Lord." (Luke 1:13-17 NIV)

"With all of my heart, I wanted to believe him. But I had given up on that prayer many years ago."

Zechariah asked the angel, "How can I be sure of this? I am an old man and my wife is well along in years." The angel answered, "I am Gabriel. I stand in the presence of God, and I have been sent to speak to you and to tell you this good news. And now you will be silent and not able to speak until the day this happens, because you did not believe my words, which will come true at their proper time." (Luke 1:18-20 NIV)

"When I realized that I could not speak, I realized that I was not being punished, but that this was a sign. Elizabeth and I were going to be parents to the forerunner of the Messiah."

When the reading of the Word came to an end, the three people in that modest dwelling were completely overwhelmed with the delight of the Lord. They were the only three people who knew that their Redeemer was on His way!

Suddenly Mary burst into a song of praise while Elizabeth, though heavy with child, began to wave her arms and clap her hands. No one would have accused Zechariah of being old the way he danced across the room. It was delightful!

In the coming days, Zechariah would share numerous scriptures of prophecy with Mary about her son—Israel's deliverer—who grew inside her.

In the Old Testament, there are over 300 Scriptures that refer to the first coming of Jesus all made hundreds of years before His birth and fulfilled to the letter. When God gave Elizabeth to Mary, He also gave her Zechariah, a priest who could teach and infuse her life with scriptural prophecy and prepare the mother of the Messiah. Never let God cease to amaze you!

TRAVEL DIARY

Do you wonder if Jesus will return during your life time? Write your thoughts below.

_____

_____

Read Matthew 24, verses 36-44. Record some specific instructions believers are to do.

_____

_____

How are you preparing for His return?

_____

_____

While we do not know when He will return as believers we know He will.

Are you looking forward to that day? _____

TRAVELING MERCIES

Father,
I am delighted that You are sending Jesus to come again! Whether or not I will be here to witness it does not matter. Because I am Your child, I will dwell with You. Help me to delight in Your Word and share it with others. Amen.

SNAPSHOT

"For the Lord himself will descend from heaven with a shout, with the voice of the archangel, and with the trump of God; and the dead in Christ shall rise first; then we which are alive and remain shall be caught up together with them in the clouds, to meet the Lord in the air; and so shall we ever be with the Lord" (1 Thessalonians 4:16-17 KJV).

WEEK 7, DAY 4
DELIGHTING IN GOD MY FATHER

SIGHTSEEING

I am in the throes of midlife. While there are many things I miss about my youth, there is a lot to be said about midlife! In some ways I like being an empty-nester. No more carpool, science projects, teacher's conferences, or trips to Disney World. It was fabulous for a season, but I'm enjoying this new season. In midlife, you realize that you have more experience, and less expectation of others, and have (hopefully!) developed a greater appreciation of ordinary things. But for me, I have the joy of being a grandma!

Surely, you saw that coming! You didn't think we would travel these many miles without at least one grandma story, did you? In case you haven't heard, let me share a secret with you. Grandparents are the most obnoxious people on the planet. I can say that because I am one! We're not offended by it either.

Out of my love for you, after these many weeks of travel, I will keep my grandma story short. My only regret is that you cannot see how precious my Maddie really is. I know other grandmas tell you how precious their grandchild is, but they haven't seen Maddie. Just take my word for it—she's a doll baby.

Maddie was ten months old and had just learned to walk. Now that's not bragging; that's a fact! It was a Friday afternoon, and her parents had stopped by for a surprise visit. When they opened my back door, they put her down when they saw me coming down the hall to greet them. On wobbly legs, she started to make her way toward me. The closer she got to her Nana, the more excited she became. As Maddie fixed her blues eyes on me she began squealing in a language that only she understood but was delightful to her Nana. She was so anxious to get to me that she tried to run. I did not move but remained in my place, allowing this beautiful child to enjoy her moment of anticipation. Finally, she got to me, stopped, looked up at me, and threw up her arms. It was like she was saying, "I'm here, Nana! I know you've been waiting for me! I'm finally here!"

She was right! I scooped her up into my arms and held her tight. I was delighted to see her. Even for this ten-month-old baby there was not a shred of doubt that her Nana loved her or was thrilled by her presence.

That's exactly how your heavenly Father feels about you! In fact, He is crazy about you! He desires that we run to Him often, sit a spell, and delight in Him.

CONVERSATIONS

It is hard for us to comprehend that the Creator of the universe cares so deeply and loves us so passionately, but He does. Do you forget that? I do. I make so many mistakes and feel so inadequate. I even forget that He created me for a relationship—not to be perfect. When you were born, God saw something in you that no one else could see—your future.

> Your eyes saw my unformed body. All the days ordained for me were written in your book before one of them came to be. (Psalm 139:16 NIV)

God knew the many ways that He would use you as a vessel to delight Him and bless others. He knew the lives that would be touched by your graciousness, kindness, and tenderness. From the very moment He breathed life into you, He delighted in you.

> You are worthy, our Lord and God, to receive glory and honor and power, for you created all things and by your will they were created and have their being. (Revelation 4:11 IV)

When you consider the above verse, knowing that it refers to you, how does that make you feel?

_____

_____

Zechariah 2:8 NIV refers to us as the "apple of his eye." And in Jeremiah 31:3 NIV, we are told,

> "I have loved you with an everlasting love; I have drawn you with loving-kindness."

And the verse that most demonstrates God's love is John 3:16 NIV:

> For God so loved the world that he gave his one and only Son, that whoever believes in him shall not perish but have eternal life.

Mary, Elizabeth, and Zachariah delighted in their God. There was no time to doubt and question, "Why did God choose me?" They could ponder night after night why they, of all people, were chosen to fulfill His promises. They instead had such an unshakable faith and belief in God that they took Him at His word. When we do that, my friend, we can delight in being His child!

If we are going to delight in and enjoy the relationship that God desires for us, then we too must take Him at His word. If we doubt, then it will rob us of the joy that Christ died for us to have.

If Maddie had doubted that her Nana loved her, she would have lacked the confidence to run to me and we both would have missed an incredible moment.

I have had some incredible moments with God. He is a loving God who loves His children. Sometimes, God seeks *me* out. But some of my best moments have been when I do what Maddie did—run to the one I know loves me!

During our study, we discussed that before we can truly enjoy healthy relation-ships with others, we must have a relationship with Him. I want to encourage you to go deeper in your relationship and delight with Him—a delight so deep that when you wake up in the morning, He is the first thought of your day, and you can enjoy the sunrise, created to make your day more beautiful!

Why not just do what Maddie did—run to the God who delights in you, throw up your hands, and just delight in Him. Enjoy Him! Don't be afraid to take Him at His Word. He says that He loves you. Believe Him!

TRAVEL DIARY

What are some ways that you can delight in your relationship with God today?

_____

_____

_____

Why do you think the God of the universe created us for relationship?

_____

_____

_____

Does your time with God feel more like duty or devotion? _____

Do you enjoy your time with God, or is it a struggle? _____

Do you ever laugh out loud with God? _____

If not, invite Him into the humorous moments of your life.

Write down three action steps that you can take today to show God how you delight in your relationship with Him.

1. _____

2. _____

3. _____

 ## TRAVELING MERCIES

> *Dear Father,*
> *So often, I get too caught up in who I am and not who You are. Help me to remember that I am your well-loved child. Father, I will delight myself with the knowledge that You created me for Your pleasure and Your purpose. I pray that I will delight Your heart today and that all the days of my life will bring You honor. Let's just "sit a spell" Father, just the two of us, and delight in our relationship. I'll go first …*

Now, take your journal and write the Lord a love letter: Sign it, the one you love.

SNAPSHOT

"The Lord directs the steps of the godly. He delights in every detail of their lives (Psalm 37:23 NLT).

Goodbyes—
Final Departure

As William Shakespeare put it, "Parting is such sweet sorrow…" That's how I'm feeling today. More often than not, goodbyes are difficult even when expected. Yet, there's a twinge of sweetness that comes from good memories and what will still be a connection deep in our hearts with that person.

Today our journey will end, and I am saying "goodbye" to you. Although I may not have met you in person, we have traveled many miles together during these seven weeks. It has been a joy to venture up and down the pages of God's Word with you. I pray you have a greater understanding of the high calling of friendship, and a deeper respect for two women who taught us what true friendship means in the body of Christ.

Before I share my final thoughts, and we say goodbye (for now) to Mary and Elizabeth, let's review some things that we learned.

For our study, we used the word F.R.I.E.N.D. as an acronym. Each letter represented a virtue that Mary and Elizabeth demonstrated. Our goal each week was to develop that virtue in our own lives and friendships. We discovered that if we are going to be women who reach others for Christ we must be:

Women of	Faith
Women who	Revere God
Women of	Integrity
Women who	Encourage others
Women who	Nurture
Women who	Delight in God

My friend, if we can apply this consistently, I have no doubt we can become the Elizabeths and Marys of the 21st century!

You can be an Elizabeth in your circle of influence by preparing women for the second coming of Christ.

You can be a Mary in your circle of influence by bringing Christ into their world.

The best way to do both is through friendship!

Now, let's roll back the pages of history one more time and consider once more the friendship of Elizabeth and Mary. As with many friendships, the time came for them to say goodbye to the close intimacy they had shared. For the purposes of building God's kingdom, it was not His will that they serve side-by-side forever. Their three months together had strengthened and equipped them for the call on their lives. I pray our weeks together have helped you as well.

The sun awakened her after a night of only fitful dozing. Today, Mary must return to Galilee. She knew this moment would come, but it didn't make it any easier. The idea of saying "goodbye" to Elizabeth and leaving the secure, comfortable environment of Elizabeth's home was already bringing the sting of tears to her eyes. Not only would she be leaving a soul mate, she would be leaving baby John—the child that the angel said would be a joy and a delight, the one who would prepare the way for *her* son.

She must also say farewell to Zechariah, the old priest who had shared his vast knowledge of scriptures concerning the coming Messiah. She had come to love and respect him deeply. His loyalty to God amazed her. The way he looked at his beloved Elizabeth made her wonder, "Will Joseph ever look at me like that?"

But the time had come. She had to get back and see Joseph. She was uncertain of what his reaction would be. But, she was certain of one thing: nothing is impossible with God. The life growing inside her was proof of that.

Mary thought about the things she wanted to say to Elizabeth, but where would she begin? What do you say to the woman who taught you about marriage, childbirth, and sacrifice? What do you say to a woman who knew you were carrying the Christ child before you told her?

Mary was so overcome with emotion that she didn't dare think too long. She didn't want to face the unpleasant fact that she might never see Elizabeth again. Afraid to trust herself to speak, she quickly penned a note and put it on Elizabeth's favorite chair.

As she put the last piece of clothing into her bag, she heard John cry. Soon, she thought, it would be her baby who would cry. That hope would make the trip home bearable.

Elizabeth had gotten up early with the baby. She asked Zechariah to pen a note to Mary, in case she was resting when she left. How would she say goodbye to this young girl who had so inspired her? What courage and faith she had! What a privilege it had been to comfort her, to protect her, and to laugh with her these months as they both anticipated God's great calls on their lives.

Elizabeth turned to Zechariah who was beginning to write …

Most Highly Favored One,

How I wish that Jehovah God would allow us to raise our sons together, but this is not His plan. I will not question Him. He is Lord. He is Yahweh, the Great and Mighty One.

I will never forget the moment I opened the door and saw you. As you entered our home, the Holy Spirit entered me. I saw with spiritual eyes that the mother of my Lord was standing before me. At that moment, I realized that we were living proof that Jehovah God had not forgotten His people.

I want to thank you for your beautiful gift of friendship. I desperately needed a friend and God provided—far beyond anything I could have imagined!

Remember the things we talked about, little one. You are God's choice—the mother of His Son. Never question, never doubt. Give Joseph time and space, and allow Jehovah to do His work. Hold fast to what the angel told you. It will get you through the most difficult days. Never be afraid to wait on God. He honors prayers!

You will always have a place here in our home. Visit when you can.

With much love, Elizabeth

Quietly, Mary slipped away the note from Elizabeth and the scroll from Zechariah with the words of the prophet Isaiah tucked safely near her heart. They would serve as a reminder of their precious time together. As she moved closer to Galilee, she realized she was somehow different. She had more confidence and a much stronger faith unlike anything she had ever experienced. Her time with Elizabeth had helped her understand and accept God's plan and divine calling. He would take care of everything.

And, He did.

Six months later, in the city of David when the pains of childbirth began, Mary recalled all that her beloved Elizabeth had taught her. She realized again God's great love and His tender mercy by providing Elizabeth to prepare her for motherhood.

During the process, she spoke to her carpenter husband with authority and experience, telling him what to expect. She had committed every detail from John's birth to memory. Beneath a star-filled sky in a lowly stable, she brought the Son of God into the world.

Now my friend, it's our turn. We must bring Christ into our world. The most effective way to do this is through friendship—true friendship, the kind that Mary and Elizabeth have modeled for us. Are you ready? I believe you are.

BONUS MILES

I could not end our journey without commenting about the two sons of the women we have grown to love. I think they would like that.

Scripture teaches us that Elizabeth's son John was the evangelist who preached, "Repent, the Lamb of God is coming!" (See Matthew 3:11). It is estimated that he may have reached as many as 300,000 people with his wilderness ministry! He also touched those in government circles, with tax collectors and Roman soldiers coming to him and accepting his message. It happened exactly as the angel Gabriel told Zechariah it would. John's greatest moment came when he baptized Jesus. Later, John was beheaded for his outspoken faith and devotion.

Mary experienced much of the extraordinary and miraculous events of her Son's ministry. She witnessed His death at Calvary but also His ascension to heaven on the Mount of Olives.

Now both women are in heaven with their sons, and their God!

So what have we learned on our journey together? Why do we need girlfriends? I truly believe because friendship is God's idea. To fully thrive and live life abundantly, we need others. So you go, girl...and make yourself some girlfriends, and by all means count me as one!

> Being confident of this, that he who began a good work in you will carry it on to completion until the day of Christ Jesus (Philippians 1:6 NIV).

We are friends forever,

—Frankie

To contact Frankie and share your friendship stories please go to her website at www.frankiedsherman.com

If you would like to use this book as a group study for the women of your church, go to Frankie's website and download a free group leaders instruction guide.

CREDITS

Chapter One

1. Billy Graham, *The Baptist Courier,* August 23, 2007, Volume 139– Number 17.

Chapter Two

1. *When a Woman Discovers Her Dream Finding God's Purpose for Your Life,* Cindi McMenamin, Harvest House Publishers: Eugene, Oregon, 2005.

Chapter 4

1. *The Purpose Driven Life,* Rick Warren, Zondervan: Grand Rapids, MI, 2002.

2. *Promises & Prayers for Friends,* Family Christian Press: Grand Rapids, MI, 2005, Charles Swindoll, page 115.

Chapter 5

1. *Encourage Me—Caring Words for Heavy Hearts,* Charles Swindoll, Zondervan: Grand Rapids, MI, 1993.

Chapter 6

1. *A Woman's High Calling: 10 Essentials For Godly Living,* Elizabeth George, Harvest House Publishers: Eugene, Oregon, 2001.

2. *Woman to Woman Mentoring,* Janet Thompson LifeWay Press: Nashville, Tennessee, 2000.

Goodbyes

1. William Shakespeare, *Romeo and Juliet,* Scene II.